Ninja Foodi Digital Air Fry Oven Cookbook 2021

1000-Day Easier & Crispier Air Crisp, Air Roast, Air Broil, Bake, Dehydrate, Toast and More Recipes for Beginners and Advanced Users

Robin Brickner

TABLE OF CONTENTS

Introduction

What is Ninja Foodi Digital Air Fry Oven

In recent years kitchen appliances have seen a major breakthrough due to developing technology and a significant improvement in functions. The traditional cooking gadgets and appliances would offer very few functions and very too big in size, occupying much space in the kitchens. However, recently various brands have launched very advanced cooking appliances, which have indeed brought innovations in the cooking world. The most prominent cooking appliance which has gathered a strong customer base recently is the Ninja Foodi Digital Air Fry Oven. It combines various cooking functions, including air frying as a significant function.

The Ninja Foodi™ has recently introduced the Ninja Foodi Digital Air Fry Oven, and it has created a significant breakthrough in the cooking world. It provides the function of an air fryer, a toaster, and all these features are available in a considerably smaller device, which saves much of your kitchen space. The Ninja Foodi Digital Air Fry Oven has proven to be the ultimate choice for people around the globe and has got very promising reviews. The device was previously available on the official store of Ninja Foodi™, but not it is also available on online selling platforms like Amazon and Walmart. The coming portions of this book will provide you a detailed insight into the functions of the Ninja Foodi Digital Air Fry Oven, its pros, and cons.

The Functions of the Ninja Foodi Digital Air Fry Oven

The primary function of the Ninja Foodi Digital Air Fry Oven is clear from its name that is air frying. Furthermore, it can also perform other cooking functions like air roasting, dehydrating, toasting, keeping the food warm, baking, and air broiling. Considering the smaller size of the Ninja Foodi Digital Air Fry Oven, an entire chicken cannot be put inside the device. Overall, the device is very promising in its overall performance parameters. Moreover, the food cooked with the Ninja Foodi Digital Air Fry Oven is very nutritious, with the perfect aroma and a delicious taste. The overall working of the functions of the Ninja Foodi Digital Air Fry Oven is as follows:

1. Air Frying

The Ninja Foodi Digital Air Fry Oven is capable of air frying 4 pounds of food at a time. The air frying mechanism of the Ninja Foodi Digital Air Fry Oven is very capable and outstanding, which evenly air fries your food. It provides ultimate perfect crispiness to your food, and the taste is without a doubt outstanding from any traditionally air fried food.

2. Toasting

Toasting your bread with the Ninja Foodi Digital Air Fry Oven is a perfect combo. You can put in 9 slices of the regular bread available in the markets and without any squishing involved at all. The toasting function of the Ninja Foodi Digital Air Fry Oven is very efficient and toasts the bread evenly, giving your bread the ultimate brownness and texture. You can also go for toasting bagels by using the bagel settings in the Ninja Foodi Digital Air Fry Oven. Moreover, the Ninja Foodi Digital Air Fry Oven offers broth high and medium toasting settings, which can be used at your discretion.

3. Air Roasting

The Ninja Foodi Digital Air Fry Oven leaves behind all the air roasting appliances launched by the Ninja Foodi™. The Ninja Foodi Digital Air Fry Oven is the perfect companion for your sheet pan dinner that includes veggies, spices, steaks or seafood, chicken, etc. The overall air roasting time of the Ninja Foodi Digital Air Fry Oven is very. It can air roast approximately 3 pounds of ingredients in around 22 minutes precisely, which serves you a delicious sheet pan dinner of 4 servings. Without a doubt, the Ninja Foodi Digital Air Fry Oven is the master in air roasting.

4. Air Baking

You can easily bake a cake or muffin in a considerably shallow pan in the Ninja Foodi Digital Air Fry Oven. Moreover, smaller items like cookies can also be baled in the Ninja Foodi Digital Air Fry Oven in a sheet pan. However, you certainly cannot pack an entire pan or the Bundt pan in the Ninja Foodi Digital Air Fry Oven. The baking function of the Ninja Foodi Digital Air Fry Oven is considerably better than the traditional baking appliances.

5. Air Broiling

The air broiling time of the Ninja Foodi Digital Air Fry Oven is also considerably lesser. The average time to air broil a chicken breast in the Ninja Foodi Digital Air Fry Oven is approximately 20 minutes. The steaks prepared with the Ninja Foodi Digital Air Fry Oven will have the perfect texture and crisp, matching the quality of any regular air broiler. The Ninja Foodi Digital Air Fry Oven provides you with the finest searing and an unmatched taste and aroma.

6. Dehydrating

The dehydrating function of the Ninja Foodi Digital Air Fry Oven is also very remarkable. The device is considerably noiseless when performing the dehydration function. Furthermore, it perfectly dehydrates your food. The overall average time taken by the Ninja Foodi Digital Air Fry Oven to properly dehydrate your food is around 10 hours. The mechanism of dehydration is directly related to the total time of dehydration. The more time you give, the more dehydrated your food will be.

7. Keep Warm

One of the most promising functions of the Ninja Foodi Digital Air Fry Oven that it keeps your food on food-safe temperature for a considerably longer time. It is very beneficial as you don't have to reheat your food at all. The food is thoroughly preserved and perfectly warm with this function of the Ninja Foodi Digital Air Fry Oven.

Pros and Cons of the Ninja Foodi Digital Air Fry Oven

Like every appliance, the Ninja Foodi Digital Air Fry Oven also has certain advantages and weak sides. However, as a whole, the device is going to be the perfect choice for your kitchen. Some of the prominent advantages of the Ninja Foodi Digital Air Fry Oven are as follows:

- It is made from stainless steel.
- Has a digital panel to customize the settings and functions.
- It can be flipped on one side when cold to save kitchen space.
- It is noiseless, energy-efficient, and smaller in size.
- It offers various cooking accessories like an Air Frying basket, crumb tray, cooking rack, and a sheet pan.

The most prominent shortcomings of the Ninja Foodi Digital Air Fry Oven are as follows:

- It is a bit expensive than traditional toaster ovens. However, considering the function it offers, the price is fairly reasonable.
- Moreover, it can't fit in an entire chicken due to its smaller size.

Breakfast Recipes

Parmesan Eggs in Avocado Cups

Preparation Time: 10 minutes
Cooking Time: 22 minutes
Servings: 2

Ingredients:

- 1 large ripe avocado, halved and pitted
- 2 eggs
- Salt and ground black pepper, as required
- 2 tablespoons Parmesan cheese, grated
- Pinch of cayenne pepper
- 1 teaspoon fresh chives, minced

Preparation:

1. With a spoon, scoop out some of the flesh from the avocado halves to make a hole.
2. Arrange the avocado halves onto a baking pan.
3. Crack 1 egg into each avocado half and sprinkle with salt and black pepper.
4. Press "Power Button" of Ninja Foodi Digital Air Fry Oven and turn the dial to select "Air Fry" mode.
5. Press "Time Button" and again turn the dial to set the cooking time to 22 minutes.
6. Now push "Temp Button" and rotate the dial to set the temperature at 350 degrees F.
7. Press "Start/Pause" button to start.
8. When the unit beeps to show that it is preheated, open the lid and grease the air fry basket.
9. Arrange the avocado halves into the air fry basket and insert in the oven.
10. After 12 minutes of cooking, sprinkle the top of avocado halves with Parmesan cheese.
11. When cooking time is completed, open the lid and transfer the avocado halves onto a platter.
12. Sprinkle with cayenne pepper snd serve hot with the garnishing of chives.

Serving Suggestions: Serve alongside baby greens.

Variation Tip: Use ripe but firm avocado.

Nutritional Information per Serving:

Calories: 286 | **Fat:** 25.2g|**Sat Fat:** 6.1g|**Carbohydrates:** 9g|**Fiber:** 0.9g|**Sugar:** 0.9g|
Protein: 9.5g

Cloud Eggs

Preparation Time: 10 minutes
Cooking Time: 7 minutes
Servings: 2

Ingredients:

- 2 eggs, whites and yolks separated
- Pinch of salt
- Pinch of freshly ground black pepper

Preparation:

1. In a bowl, add the egg white, salt and black pepper and beat until stiff peaks form.
2. Line a baking pan with parchment paper.
3. Carefully, make a pocket in the center of each egg white circle.
4. Press "Power Button" of Ninja Foodi Digital Air Fry Oven and turn the dial to select the "Air Broil" mode.
5. Press "Time Button" and again turn the dial to set the cooking time to 7 minutes.
6. Press "Start/Pause" button to start.
7. When the unit beeps to show that it is preheated, open the lid and insert the baking pan in the oven.
8. Place 1 egg yolk into each egg white pocket after 5 minutes of cooking.
9. When cooking time is completed, open the lid and serve.

Serving Suggestions: Serve alongside toasted bread slices.

Variation Tip: Make sure to use a cleaned bowl for whipping the egg whites.

Nutritional Information per Serving:

Calories: 63 | **Fat:** 4.4g|**Sat Fat:** 1.4g|**Carbohydrates:** 0.3g|**Fiber:** 0g|**Sugar:** 0.3g| **Protein:** 5.5g

Savory Parsley Soufflé

Preparation Time: 10 minutes
Cooking Time: 8 minutes
Servings: 2

Ingredients:

- 2 tablespoons light cream
- 2 eggs
- 1 tablespoon fresh parsley, chopped
- 1 fresh red chili pepper, chopped
- Salt, as required

Preparation:

1. Grease 2 soufflé dishes.
2. In a bowl, add all the ingredients and beat until well combined.
3. Divide the mixture into prepared soufflé dishes.
4. Press "Power Button" of Ninja Foodi Digital Air Fry Oven and turn the dial to select "Air Fry" mode.
5. Press "Time Button" and again turn the dial to set the cooking time to 8 minutes.
6. Now push "Temp Button" and rotate the dial to set the temperature at 390 degrees F.
7. Press "Start/Pause" button to start.
8. When the unit beeps to show that it is preheated, open the lid and grease the air fry basket.
9. Arrange the soufflé dishes into the air fry basket and insert in the oven.
10. When cooking time is completed, open the lid and serve hot.

Serving Suggestions: Serve alongside a piece of crusty bread.

Variation Tip: You can replace chives with parsley.

Nutritional Information per Serving:

Calories: 108 | **Fat:** 9g|**Sat Fat:** 4.3g|**Carbohydrates:** 1.1g|**Fiber:** 0.22g|**Sugar:** 0.5g| **Protein:** 6g

Bacon, Spinach & Egg Cups

Preparation Time: 15 minutes
Cooking Time: 16 minutes
Servings: 3

Ingredients:

- 3 eggs
- 6 cooked bacon slices, chopped
- 2 cups fresh baby spinach
- 1/3 cup heavy cream
- 3 tablespoons Parmesan cheese, grated
- Salt and ground black pepper, as required

Preparation:

1. Heat a nonstick skillet over medium-high heat and cook the bacon for about 5 minutes.
2. Add the spinach and cook for about 2-3 minutes.
3. Stir in the heavy cream and Parmesan cheese and cook for about 2-3 minutes.
4. Remove from the heat and set aside to cool slightly.
5. Grease 3 (3-inch) ramekins.
6. Crack 1 egg in each prepared ramekin and top with bacon mixture.
7. Press "Power Button" of Ninja Foodi Digital Air Fry Oven and turn the dial to select "Air Fry" mode.
8. Press "Time Button" and again turn the dial to set the cooking time to 5 minutes.
9. Now push "Temp Button" and rotate the dial to set the temperature at 350 degrees F.
10. Press "Start/Pause" button to start.
11. When the unit beeps to show that it is preheated, open the lid and grease the air fry basket.
12. Arrange the ramekins into the air fry basket and insert in the oven.
13. When cooking time is completed, open the lid and sprinkle each ramekin with salt and black pepper.
14. Serve hot.

Serving Suggestions: Serve alongside the English muffins.

Variation Tip: Use freshly grated cheese.

Nutritional Information per Serving:

Calories: 442 | **Fat:** 34.5g|**Sat Fat:** 12.9g|**Carbohydrates:** 2.3g|**Fiber:** 0.5g|**Sugar:** 0.4g| **Protein:** 29.6g

Savory Sausage & Beans Muffins

Preparation Time: 15 minutes
Cooking Time: 20 minutes
Servings: 6

Ingredients:

- 4 eggs
- ½ cup cheddar cheese, shredded
- 3 tablespoons heavy cream
- 1 tablespoon tomato paste
- ¼ teaspoon salt
- Pinch of freshly ground black pepper
- Cooking spray
- 4 cooked breakfast sausage links, chopped
- 3 tablespoons baked beans

Preparation:

1. Grease a 6 cups muffin pan.
2. In a bowl, add the eggs, cheddar cheese, heavy cream, tomato paste, salt and black pepper and beat until well combined.
3. Stir in the sausage pieces and beans.
4. Divide the mixture into prepared muffin cups evenly.
5. Press "Power Button" of Ninja Foodi Digital Air Fry Oven and turn the dial to select "Air Bake" mode.
6. Press "Time Button" and again turn the dial to set the cooking time to 20 minutes.
7. Now push "Temp Button" and rotate the dial to set the temperature at 350 degrees F.
8. Press "Start/Pause" button to start.
9. When the unit beeps to show that it is preheated, open the lid.
10. Arrange the muffin pan over the wire rack and insert in the oven.
11. When cooking time is completed, open the lid and place the muffin pan onto a wire rack to cool for 5 minutes before serving.

Serving Suggestions: Serve with drizzling of melted butter.

Variation Tip: You can use cooked beans of your choice.

Nutritional Information per Serving:

Calories: 258 | **Fat:** 20.4g|**Sat Fat:** 9.3g|**Carbohydrates:** 4.2g|**Fiber:** 0.8g|**Sugar:** 0.9g| **Protein:** 14.6g

Mushroom Frittata

Preparation Time: 15 minutes
Cooking Time: 36 minutes
Servings: 4

Ingredients:

- 2 tablespoons olive oil
- 1 shallot, sliced thinly
- 2 garlic cloves, minced
- 4 cups white mushrooms, chopped
- 6 large eggs
- ¼ teaspoon red pepper flakes, crushed
- Salt and ground black pepper, as required
- ½ teaspoon fresh dill, minced
- ½ cup cream cheese, softened

Preparation:

1. In a skillet, heat the oil over medium heat and cook the shallot, mushrooms and garlic for about 5-6 minutes, stirring frequently.
2. Remove from the heat and transfer the mushroom mixture into a bowl.
3. In another bowl, add the eggs, red pepper flakes, salt and black peppers and beat well.
4. Add the mushroom mixture and stir to combine.
5. Place the egg mixture into a greased baking pan and sprinkle with the dill.
6. Spread cream cheese over egg mixture evenly.
7. Press "Power Button" of Ninja Foodi Digital Air Fry Oven and turn the dial to select "Air Fry" mode.
8. Press "Time Button" and again turn the dial to set the cooking time to 30 minutes.
9. Now push "Temp Button" and rotate the dial to set the temperature at 330 degrees F.
10. Press "Start/Pause" button to start.
11. When the unit beeps to show that it is preheated, open the lid.
12. Arrange pan over the wire rack and insert in the oven.
13. When cooking time is completed, open the lid and place the baking pan onto a wire rack for about 5 minutes
14. Cut into equal-sized wedges and serve.

Serving Suggestions: Serve with green salad.

Variation Tip: for better taste, let the frittata sit at room temperature for a few minutes to set before cutting.

Nutritional Information per Serving:

Calories: 290 | **Fat:** 24.8g|**Sat Fat:** 9.7g|**Carbohydrates:** 5g|**Fiber:** 0.8g|**Sugar:** 1.9g| **Protein:** 14.1g

Potato & Corned Beef Casserole

Preparation Time: 15 minutes
Cooking Time: 1 hour 20 minutes
Servings: 3

Ingredients:

- 3 Yukon Gold potatoes
- 2 tablespoons unsalted butter
- ½ of onion, chopped
- 2 garlic cloves, minced
- 2 tablespoons vegetable oil
- ½ teaspoon salt
- 12 ounces corned beef
- 3 eggs

Preparation:

1. Press "Power Button" of Ninja Foodi Digital Air Fry Oven and turn the dial to select "Air Bake" mode.
2. Press "Time Button" and again turn the dial to set the cooking time to 30 minutes.
3. Now push "Temp Button" and rotate the dial to set the temperature at 350 degrees F.
4. Press "Start/Pause" button to start.
5. When the unit beeps to show that it is preheated, open the lid and grease the air fry basket.
6. Place the potatoes into the prepared air fry basket and insert in the oven.
7. When cooking time is completed, open the lid and transfer the potatoes onto a tray.
8. Set aside to cool for about 15 minutes.
9. After cooling, cut the potatoes into ½-inch-thick slices.
10. In a skillet, melt the butter over medium heat and cook the onion and garlic for about 10 minutes.
11. Remove from the heat and place the onion mixture into a casserole dish.
12. Add the potato slices, oil salt and corned beef and mix well.
13. Press "Power Button" of Ninja Foodi Digital Air Fry Oven and turn the dial to select "Air Bake" mode.
14. Press "Time Button" and again turn the dial to set the cooking time to 40 minutes.
15. Now push "Temp Button" and rotate the dial to set the temperature at 350 degrees F.

16. Press "Start/Pause" button to start.
17. When the unit beeps to show that it is preheated, open the lid.
18. Arrange the casserole dish over the wire rack and insert in the oven.
19. After 30 minutes of cooking, remove the casserole dish and crack 3 eggs on top.
20. When cooking time is completed, open the lid and serve immediately.

Serving Suggestions: Serve with fresh baby kale.

Variation Tip: cut the potatoes in equal-sized slices.

Nutritional Information per Serving:

Calories: 542 | **Fat:** 35.6g|**Sat Fat:** 14.1g|**Carbohydrates:** 33.1g|**Fiber:** 2.8g|**Sugar:** 2.3g| **Protein:** 24.7g

Simple Bread

Preparation Time: 15 minutes
Cooking Time: 18 minutes
Servings: 4

Ingredients:

- 7/8 cup whole-wheat flour
- 7/8 cup plain flour
- 1¾ ounces pumpkin seeds
- 1 teaspoon salt
- ½ of sachet instant yeast
- ½-1 cup lukewarm water

Preparation:

1. In a bowl, mix together the flours, pumpkin seeds, salt and yeast and mix well.
2. Slowly, add the desired amount of water and mix until a soft dough ball forms.
3. With your hands, knead the dough until smooth and elastic.
4. Place the dough ball into a bowl.
5. With a plastic wrap, cover the bowl and set aside in a warm place for 30 minutes or until doubled in size.
6. Press "Power Button" of Ninja Foodi Digital Air Fry Oven and turn the dial to select "Air Fry" mode.
7. Press "Time Button" and again turn the dial to set the cooking time to 18 minutes.
8. Now push "Temp Button" and rotate the dial to set the temperature at 350 degrees F.
9. Press "Start/Pause" button to start.
10. Place the dough ball in a greased cake pan and brush the top of the dough with water.
11. When the unit beeps to show that it is preheated, open the lid.
12. Place the cake pan into the air fry basket and insert in the oven.
13. When cooking time is completed, open the lid and place the pan onto a wire rack for about 10-15 minutes.
14. Carefully, invert the bread onto the wire rack to cool completely cool before slicing.
15. Cut the bread into desired sized slices and serve.

Serving Suggestions: Serve with your favorite jam.

Variation Tip: Don't use hot water.

Nutritional Information per Serving:

Calories: 268 | **Fat:** 6g|**Sat Fat:** 1.1g|**Carbohydrates:** 43.9g|**Fiber:** 2.5g|**Sugar:** 1.1g| **Protein:** 9.2g

Date Bread

Preparation Time: 15 minutes
Cooking Time: 22 minutes
Servings: 10

Ingredients:

- 2½ cup dates, pitted and chopped
- ¼ cup butter
- 1 cup hot water
- 1½ cups flour
- ½ cup brown sugar
- 1 teaspoon baking powder
- 1 teaspoon baking soda
- ½ teaspoon salt
- 1 egg

Preparation:

1. In a large bowl, add the dates, butter and top with the hot water. Set aside for about 5 minutes.
2. In a separate bowl, mix together the flour, brown sugar, baking powder, baking soda, and salt.
3. In the same bowl of dates, add the flour mixture and egg and mix well.
4. Grease a non-stick loaf pan.
5. Place the mixture into the prepared pan.
6. Press "Power Button" of Ninja Foodi Digital Air Fry Oven and turn the dial to select "Air Fry" mode.
7. Press "Time Button" and again turn the dial to set the cooking time to 22 minutes.
8. Now push "Temp Button" and rotate the dial to set the temperature at 340 degrees F.
9. Press "Start/Pause" button to start.
10. When the unit beeps to show that it is preheated, open the lid.
11. Place the pan into the air fry basket and insert in the oven.
12. When cooking time is completed, open the lid and place the pan onto a wire rack for about 10-15 minutes.
13. Carefully, invert the bread onto the wire rack to cool completely cool before slicing.
14. Cut the bread into desired sized slices and serve.

Serving Suggestions: Serve these bread slices with butter.

Variation Tip: Use soft dates.

Nutritional Information per Serving:

Calories: 129 | **Fat:** 5.4g|**Sat Fat:** 3.1g|**Carbohydrates:** 55.1g|**Fiber:** 4.1g|**Sugar:** 35.3g|**Protein:** 3.6g

Sweet & Spiced Toasts

Preparation Time: 10 minutes
Cooking Time: 4   minutes
Servings: 3

Ingredients:

- ¼ cup sugar
- ½ teaspoon ground cinnamon
- 1/8 teaspoon ground cloves
- 1/8 teaspoon ground ginger
- ½ teaspoons vanilla extract
- ¼ cup salted butter, softened
- 6 bread slices

Preparation:

1. In a bowl, add the sugar, vanilla, cinnamon, pepper, and butter. Mix until smooth.
2. Spread the butter mixture evenly over each bread slice.
3. Press "Power Button" of Ninja Foodi Digital Air Fry Oven and turn the dial to select "Air Fry" mode.
4. Press "Time Button" and again turn the dial to set the cooking time to 4 minutes.
5. Now push "Temp Button" and rotate the dial to set the temperature at 400 degrees F.
6. Press "Start/Pause" button to start.
7. When the unit beeps to show that it is preheated, open the lid and grease the air fry basket.
8. Place the bread slices into the prepared air fry basket, buttered-side up. and insert in the oven.
9. Flip the slices once halfway through.
10. When cooking time is completed, open the lid and transfer the French toasts onto a platter.
11. Serve warm.

Serving Suggestions: Serve with the drizzling of maple syrup.

Variation Tip: Adjust the ratio of spices according to your taste.

Nutritional Information per Serving:

Calories: 261 | **Fat:** 12g|**Sat Fat:** 3.6g|**Carbohydrates:** 30.6g|**Fiber:** 0.3g|**Sugar:** 22.3g| **Protein:** 9.1g

Snacks & Appetizer Recipes

Roasted Peanuts

Preparation Time: 5 minutes
Cooking Time: 14 minutes
Servings: 6

Ingredients:

- 1½ cups raw peanuts
- Nonstick cooking spray

Preparation:

1. Press "Power Button" of Ninja Foodi Digital Air Fry Oven and turn the dial to select "Air Fry" mode.
2. Press "Time Button" and again turn the dial to set the cooking time to 14 minutes.
3. Now push "Temp Button" and rotate the dial to set the temperature at 320 degrees F.
4. Press "Start/Pause" button to start.
5. When the unit beeps to show that it is preheated, open the lid.
6. Arrange the peanuts in air fry basket and insert in the oven.
7. While cooking, toss the peanuts twice.
8. After 9 minutes of cooking, spray the peanuts with cooking spray.
9. When cooking time is completed, open the lid and transfer the peanuts into a heatproof bowl.
10. Serve warm.

Serving Suggestions: Serve with a sprinkling of little cinnamon.

Variation Tip: Choose raw peanuts.

Nutritional Information per Serving:

Calories: 207 | **Fat:** 18g|**Sat Fat:** 2.5g|**Carbohydrates:** 5.9g|**Fiber:** 3.1g|**Sugar:** 1.5g| **Protein:** 9.4g

Tortilla Chips

Preparation Time: 10 minutes
Cooking Time: 3 minutes
Servings: 3

Ingredients:

- 4 corn tortillas, cut into triangles
- 1 tablespoon olive oil
- Salt, to taste

Preparation:

1. Coat the tortilla chips with oil and then sprinkle each side of the tortillas with salt.
2. Press "Power Button" of Ninja Foodi Digital Air Fry Oven and turn the dial to select "Air Fry" mode.
3. Press "Time Button" and again turn the dial to set the cooking time to 3 minutes.
4. Now push "Temp Button" and rotate the dial to set the temperature at 390 degrees F.
5. Press "Start/Pause" button to start.
6. When the unit beeps to show that it is preheated, open the lid.
7. Arrange the tortilla chips in air fry basket and insert in the oven.
8. When cooking time is completed, open the lid and transfer the tortilla chips onto a platter.
9. Serve warm.

Serving Suggestions: Serve with guacamole.

Variation Tip: Use whole grain tortillas.

Nutritional Information per Serving:

Calories: 110 | **Fat:** 5.6g|**Sat Fat:** 0.8g|**Carbohydrates:** 14.3g|**Fiber:** 2g|**Sugar:** 0.3g| **Protein:** 1.8g

Zucchini Fries

Preparation Time: 10 minutes
Cooking Time: 12 minutes
Servings: 4

Ingredients:

- 1 pound zucchini, sliced into 2½-inch sticks
- Salt, as required
- 2 tablespoons olive oil
- ¾ cup panko breadcrumbs

Preparation:

1. In a colander, add the zucchini and sprinkle with salt. Set aside for about 10 minutes.
2. Gently pat dry the zucchini sticks with the paper towels and coat with oil.
3. In a shallow dish, add the breadcrumbs.
4. Coat the zucchini sticks with breadcrumbs evenly.
5. Press "Power Button" of Ninja Foodi Digital Air Fry Oven and turn the dial to select "Air Fry" mode.
6. Press "Time Button" and again turn the dial to set the cooking time to 12 minutes.
7. Now push "Temp Button" and rotate the dial to set the temperature at 400 degrees F.
8. Press "Start/Pause" button to start.
9. When the unit beeps to show that it is preheated, open the lid.
10. Arrange the zucchini fries in air fry basket and insert in the oven.
11. When cooking time is completed, open the lid and transfer the zucchini fries onto a platter.
12. Serve warm.

Serving Suggestions: Serve with ketchup.

Variation Tip: You can use breadcrumbs of your choice.

Nutritional Information per Serving:

Calories: 151 | **Fat:** 8.6g|**Sat Fat:** 1.6g|**Carbohydrates:** 6.9g|**Fiber:** 1.3g|**Sugar:** 2g| **Protein:** 1.9g

Cod Nuggets

Preparation Time: 15 minutes
Cooking Time: 18 minutes
Servings: 5

Ingredients:

- 1 cup all-purpose flour
- 2 eggs
- ¾ cup breadcrumbs
- Pinch of salt
- 2 tablespoons olive oil
- 1 pound cod, cut into 1x2½-inch strips

Preparation:

1. In a shallow dish, place the flour.
2. Crack the eggs in a second dish and beat well.
3. In a third dish, mix together the breadcrumbs, salt and oil.
4. Coat the nuggets with flour, then dip into beaten eggs and finally, coat with the breadcrumbs.
5. Press "Power Button" of Ninja Foodi Digital Air Fry Oven and turn the dial to select "Air Fry" mode.
6. Press "Time Button" and again turn the dial to set the cooking time to 8 minutes.
7. Now push "Temp Button" and rotate the dial to set the temperature at 390 degrees F.
8. Press "Start/Pause" button to start.
9. When the unit beeps to show that it is preheated, open the lid.
10. Arrange the nuggets in air fry basket and insert in the oven.
11. When cooking time is completed, open the lid and transfer the nuggets onto a platter.
12. Serve warm.

Serving Suggestions: Enjoy with tartar sauce.

Variation Tip: Use fresh fish.

Nutritional Information per Serving:

Calories: 323 | **Fat:** 9.2g|**Sat Fat:** 1.7g|**Carbohydrates:** 30.9g|**Fiber:** 1.4g|**Sugar:** 1.2g| **Protein:** 27.7g

Glazed Chicken Wings

Preparation Time: 15 minutes
Cooking Time: 25 minutes
Servings: 4

Ingredients:

- 1½ pounds chicken wingettes and drumettes
- 1/3 cup tomato sauce
- 2 tablespoons balsamic vinegar
- 2 tablespoons maple syrup
- ½ teaspoon liquid smoke
- ¼ teaspoon red pepper flakes, crushed
- Salt, as required

Preparation:

1. Arrange the wings onto the greased sheet pan.
2. Press "Power Button" of Ninja Foodi Digital Air Fry Oven and turn the dial to select "Air Fry" mode.
3. Press "Time Button" and again turn the dial to set the cooking time to 25 minutes.
4. Now push "Temp Button" and rotate the dial to set the temperature at 380 degrees F.
5. Press "Start/Pause" button to start.
6. When the unit beeps to show that it is preheated, open the lid and insert the sheet pan in oven.
7. Meanwhile, in a small pan, add the remaining ingredients over medium heat and cook for about 10 minutes, stirring occasionally.
8. When cooking time is completed, open the lid and place the chicken wings into a bowl.
9. Add the sauce and toss to coat well.
10. Serve immediately.

Serving Suggestions: Serve with your favorite dip.

Variation Tip: Honey can replace the maple syrup.

Nutritional Information per Serving:

Calories: 356 | **Fat:** 12.7g | **Sat Fat:** 3.5g | **Carbohydrates:** 7.9g | **Fiber:** 0.3g | **Sugar:** 6.9g | **Protein:** 49.5g

Beef Taquitos

Preparation Time: 15 minutes
Cooking Time: 8 minutes
Servings: 6

Ingredients:

- 6 corn tortillas
- 2 cups cooked beef, shredded
- ½ cup onion, chopped
- 1 cup pepper jack cheese, shredded
- Olive oil cooking spray

Preparation:

1. Arrange the tortillas onto a smooth surface.
2. Place the shredded meat over one corner of each tortilla, followed by onion and cheese.
3. Roll each tortilla to secure the filling and secure with toothpicks.
4. Spray each taquito with cooking spray evenly.
5. Arrange the taquitos onto the greased sheet pan.
6. Place the tofu mixture in the greased sheet pan.
7. Press "Power Button" of Ninja Foodi Digital Air Fry Oven and turn the dial to select "Air Fry" mode.
8. Press "Time Button" and again turn the dial to set the cooking time to 8 minutes.
9. Now push "Temp Button" and rotate the dial to set the temperature at 400 degrees F.
10. Press "Start/Pause" button to start.
11. When the unit beeps to show that it is preheated, open the lid and insert the sheet pan in oven.
12. When cooking time is completed, open the lid and
13. When cooking time is completed, open the lid and transfer the taquitos onto a platter.
14. Serve warm.

Serving Suggestions: Serve with yogurt dip.

Variation Tip: you can use any kind of cooked meat in this recipe.

Nutritional Information per Serving:

Calories: 228| **Fat:** 9.6g|**Sat Fat:** 4.8g|**Carbohydrates:** 12.3g|**Fiber:** 1.7g|**Sugar:** 0.6g| **Protein:** 22.7g

Potato Croquettes

Preparation Time: 15 minutes
Cooking Time: 8 minutes
Servings: 4

Ingredients:

- 2 medium Russet potatoes, peeled and cubed
- 2 tablespoons all-purpose flour
- ½ cup Parmesan cheese, grated
- 1 egg yolk
- 2 tablespoons fresh chives, minced
- Pinch of ground nutmeg
- Salt and freshly ground black pepper, as needed
- 2 eggs
- ½ cup breadcrumbs
- 2 tablespoons vegetable oil

Preparation:

1. In a pan of a boiling water, add the potatoes and cook for about 15 minutes.
2. Drain the potatoes well and transfer into a large bowl.
3. With a potato masher, mash the potatoes and set aside to cool completely.
4. In the bowl of mashed potatoes, add the flour, Parmesan cheese, egg yolk, chives, nutmeg, salt, and black pepper and mix until well combined.
5. Make small equal-sized balls from the mixture.
6. Now, roll each ball into a cylinder shape.
7. In a shallow dish, crack the eggs and beat well.
8. In another dish, mix together the breadcrumbs and oil.
9. Dip the croquettes in egg mixture and then coat with the breadcrumbs mixture.
10. Press "Power Button" of Ninja Foodi Digital Air Fry Oven and turn the dial to select "Air Fry" mode.
11. Press "Time Button" and again turn the dial to set the cooking time to 8 minutes.
12. Now push "Temp Button" and rotate the dial to set the temperature at 390 degrees F.
13. Press "Start/Pause" button to start.
14. When the unit beeps to show that it is preheated, open the lid.
15. Arrange the croquettes in air fry basket and insert in the oven.
16. When cooking time is completed, open the lid and transfer the croquettes onto a platter.
17. Serve warm.

Serving Suggestions: Serve with mustard sauce.

Variation Tip: Make sure to use dried breadcrumbs.

Nutritional Information per Serving:

Calories: 283 | **Fat:** 13.4g|**Sat Fat:** 3.8g|**Carbohydrates:** 29.9g|**Fiber:** 3.3g|**Sugar:** 2.3g| **Protein:** 11.5g

Cauliflower Poppers

Preparation Time: 10 minutes
Cooking Time: 20 minutes
Servings: 6

Ingredients:

- 3 tablespoons olive oil
- 1 teaspoon paprika
- ½ teaspoon ground cumin
- ¼ teaspoon ground turmeric
- Salt and ground black pepper, as required
- 1 medium head cauliflower, cut into florets

Preparation:

1. In a bowl, place all ingredients and toss to coat well.
2. Place the cauliflower mixture in the greased sheet pan.
3. Press "Power Button" of Ninja Foodi Digital Air Fry Oven and turn the dial to select the "Air Bake" mode.
4. Press "Time Button" and again turn the dial to set the cooking time to 20 minutes.
5. Now push "Temp Button" and rotate the dial to set the temperature at 450 degrees F.
6. Press "Start/Pause" button to start.
7. When the unit beeps to show that it is preheated, open the lid and insert the sheet pan in oven.
8. Flip the cauliflower mixture once halfway through.
9. When cooking time is completed, open the lid and transfer the cauliflower poppers onto a platter.
10. Serve warm.

Serving Suggestions: Serve with a squeeze of lemon juice.

Variation Tip: Feel free to use spices of your choice.

Nutritional Information per Serving:

Calories: 73 | **Fat:** 7.1g|**Sat Fat:** 1g|**Carbohydrates:** 2.7g|**Fiber:** 1.3g|**Sugar:** 1.1g| **Protein:** 1g

Spicy Spinach Chips

Preparation Time: 10 minutes
Cooking Time: 10 minutes
Servings: 4

Ingredients:

- 2 cups fresh spinach leaves, torn into bite-sized pieces
- ½ tablespoon coconut oil, melted
- 1/8 teaspoon garlic powder
- Salt, as required

Preparation:

1. In a large bowl and mix together all the ingredients.
2. Arrange the spinach pieces onto the greased sheet pan.
3. Press "Power Button" of Ninja Foodi Digital Air Fry Oven and turn the dial to select "Air Fry" mode.
4. Press "Time Button" and again turn the dial to set the cooking time to 10 minutes.
5. Now push "Temp Button" and rotate the dial to set the temperature at 300 degrees F.
6. Press "Start/Pause" button to start.
7. When the unit beeps to show that it is preheated, open the lid.
8. Insert the sheet pan in oven.
9. Toss the spinach chips once halfway through.
10. When cooking time is completed, open the lid and transfer the spinach chips onto a platter.
11. Serve warm.

Serving Suggestions: Serve with a sprinkling of cayenne pepper.

Variation Tip: Make sure to pat dry the spinach leaves before using.

Nutritional Information per Serving:

Calories: 18 | **Fat:** 1.5g|**Sat Fat:** 0g|**Carbohydrates:** 0.5g|**Fiber:** 0.3g|**Sugar:** 0.1g| **Protein:** 0.5g

Persimmon Chips

Preparation Time: 10 minutes
Cooking Time: 10 minutes
Servings: 2

Ingredients:

- 2 ripe persimmons, cut into slices horizontally
- Salt and ground black pepper, as required

Preparation:

1. Arrange the persimmons slices onto the greased sheet pan.
2. Press "Power Button" of Ninja Foodi Digital Air Fry Oven and turn the dial to select "Air Fry" mode.
3. Press "Time Button" and again turn the dial to set the cooking time to 10 minutes.
4. Now push "Temp Button" and rotate the dial to set the temperature at 400 degrees F.
5. Press "Start/Pause" button to start.
6. When the unit beeps to show that it is preheated, open the lid.
7. Insert the sheet pan in oven.
8. Flip the chips once halfway through.
9. When cooking time is completed, open the lid and transfer the chips onto a platter.
10. Serve warm.

Serving Suggestions: Serve with a sprinkling of ground cinnamon.

Variation Tip: You can use these chips in a homemade trail mix.

Nutritional Information per Serving:

Calories: 32 | **Fat:** 0.1g|**Sat Fat:** 0g|**Carbohydrates:** 8.4g|**Fiber:** 0g|**Sugar:** 0g| **Protein:** 0.2g

Vegetable & Sides Recipes

Stuffed Zucchini

Preparation Time: 20 minutes
Cooking Time: 35 minutes
Servings: 4

Ingredients:

- 2 zucchinis, cut in half lengthwise
- ½ teaspoon garlic powder
- Salt, as required
- 1 teaspoon olive oil
- 4 ounces fresh mushrooms, chopped
- 4 ounces carrots, peeled and shredded
- 3 ounces onion, chopped
- 4 ounces goat cheese, crumbled
- 12 fresh basil leaves
- ½ teaspoon onion powder

Preparation:

1. Carefully, scoop the flesh from the middle of each zucchini half.
2. Season each zucchini half with a little garlic powder and salt.
3. Arrange the zucchini halves into the greased baking pan.
4. Place the oat mixture over salmon fillets and gently, press down.
5. Press "Power Button" of Ninja Foodi Digital Air Fry Oven and turn the dial to select the "Air Bake" mode.
6. Press "Time Button" and again turn the dial to set the cooking time to 20 minutes.
7. Now push "Temp Button" and rotate the dial to set the temperature at 450 degrees F.
8. Press "Start/Pause" button to start.
9. When the unit beeps to show that it is preheated, open the lid.
10. Insert the baking pan in oven.
11. Meanwhile, in a skillet, heat the oil over medium heat and cook the mushrooms, carrots, onions, onion powder and salt and cook for about 5-6 minutes.
12. Remove from the heat and set aside.
13. Remove the baking pan from oven and set aside.
14. Stuff each zucchini half with veggie mixture and top with basil leaves, followed by the cheese.
15. Press "Power Button" of Ninja Foodi Digital Air Fry Oven and turn the dial to select the "Air Bake" mode.
16. Press "Time Button" and again turn the dial to set the cooking time to 15 minutes.
17. Now push "Temp Button" and rotate the dial to set the temperature at 450 degrees F.

18. Press "Start/Pause" button to start.
19. When the unit beeps to show that it is preheated, open the lid.
20. Insert the baking pan in oven.
21. When cooking time is completed, open the lid and transfer the zucchini halves onto a platter.
22. Serve warm.

Serving Suggestions: Serve alongside fresh grens.

Variation Tip: Any kind of cheese can be used in this recipe.

Nutritional Information per Serving:

Calories: 181 | **Fat:** 11.6g|**Sat Fat:** 7.2g|**Carbohydrates:** 10.1g|**Fiber:** 2.6g|**Sugar:** 5.3g| **Protein:** 11.3g

Tofu in Sweet & Sour Sauce

Preparation Time: 20 minutes
Cooking Time: 20 minutes
Servings: 4

Ingredients:

For Tofu:

- 1 (14-ounce) block firm tofu, pressed and cubed
- ½ cup arrowroot flour
- ½ teaspoon sesame oil

For Sauce:

- 4 tablespoons low-sodium soy sauce
- 1½ tablespoons rice vinegar
- 1½ tablespoons chili sauce
- 1 tablespoon agave nectar
- 2 large garlic cloves, minced

- 1 teaspoon fresh ginger, peeled and grated
- 2 scallions (green part), chopped

Preparation:

1. In a bowl, mix together the tofu, arrowroot flour, and sesame oil.
2. Press "Power Button" of Ninja Foodi Digital Air Fry Oven and turn the dial to select "Air Fry" mode.
3. Press "Time Button" and again turn the dial to set the cooking time to 20 minutes.
4. Now push "Temp Button" and rotate the dial to set the temperature at 360 degrees F.
5. Press "Start/Pause" button to start.
6. When the unit beeps to show that it is preheated, open the lid.
7. Arrange the tofu cubes in greased air fry basket and insert in the oven.
8. Flip the tofu cubes once halfway through.
9. Meanwhile, for the sauce: in a bowl, add all the ingredients except scallions and beat until well combined.
10. When cooking time is completed, open the lid and remove the tofu.
11. Transfer the tofu into a skillet with sauce over medium heat and cook for about 3 minutes, stirring occasionally.
12. Garnish with scallions and serve hot.

Serving Suggestions: Serve with plain boiled rice.

Variation Tip: s

Nutritional Information per Serving:

Calories: 115 | **Fat:** 4.8g|**Sat Fat:** 1g|**Carbohydrates:** 10.2g|**Fiber:** 1.7g|**Sugar:** 5.6g| **Protein:** 0.1g

Tofu with Broccoli

Preparation Time: 15 minutes
Cooking Time: 15 minutes
Servings: 3

Ingredients:

- 8 ounces firm tofu, drained, pressed and cubed
- 1 head broccoli, cut into florets
- 1 tablespoon butter, melted
- 1 teaspoon ground turmeric
- ¼ teaspoon paprika
- Salt and ground black pepper, as required

Preparation:

1. In a bowl, mix together all ingredients.
2. Place the tofu mixture in the greased cooking pan.
3. Press "Power Button" of Ninja Foodi Digital Air Fry Oven and turn the dial to select "Air Fry" mode.
4. Press "Time Button" and again turn the dial to set the cooking time to 15 minutes.
5. Now push "Temp Button" and rotate the dial to set the temperature at 390 degrees F.
6. Press "Start/Pause" button to start.
7. When the unit beeps to show that it is preheated, open the lid.
8. Insert the baking pan in oven.
9. Toss the tofu mixture once halfway through.
10. When cooking time is completed, open the lid and serve hot.

Serving Suggestions: Serve with cooked pasta.

Variation Tip: Don't forget to drain the tofu completely.

Nutritional Information per Serving:

Calories: 119 | **Fat:** 7.4g|**Sat Fat:** 3.1g|**Carbohydrates:** 7.5g|**Fiber:** 3.1g|**Sugar:** 1.9g| **Protein:** 8.7g

Veggie Rice

Preparation Time: 15 minutes
Cooking Time: 18 minutes
Servings: 2

Ingredients:

- 2 cups cooked white rice
- 1 tablespoon vegetable oil
- 2 teaspoons sesame oil, toasted and divided
- 1 tablespoon water
- Salt and ground white pepper, as required
- 1 large egg, lightly beaten
- ½ cup frozen peas, thawed
- ½ cup frozen carrots, thawed
- 1 teaspoon soy sauce
- 1 teaspoon Sriracha sauce
- ½ teaspoon sesame seeds, toasted

Preparation:

1. In a large bowl, add the rice, vegetable oil, one teaspoon of sesame oil, water, salt, and white pepper and mix well.
2. Transfer rice mixture into a lightly greased baking pan.
3. Press "Power Button" of Ninja Foodi Digital Air Fry Oven and turn the dial to select "Air Fry" mode.
4. Press "Time Button" and again turn the dial to set the cooking time to 18 minutes.
5. Now push "Temp Button" and rotate the dial to set the temperature at 380 degrees F.
6. Press "Start/Pause" button to start.
7. When the unit beeps to show that it is preheated, open the lid.
8. Place the pan over the wire rack and insert in the oven.
9. While cooking, stir the mixture once after 12 minutes.
10. After 12 minutes of cooking, press "Start/Pause" to pause cooking.
11. Remove the pan from oven and place the beaten egg over rice.
12. Again, insert the pan in the oven and press "Start/Pause" to resume cooking.
13. After 16 minutes of cooking, press "Start/Pause" to pause cooking.
14. Remove the pan from and stir in the peas and carrots.
15. Again, insert the pan in the oven and press "Start/Pause" to resume cooking.
16. Meanwhile, in a bowl, mix together the soy sauce, Sriracha sauce, sesame seeds and the remaining sesame oil.
17. When cooking time is completed, open the lid and transfer the rice mixture into a serving bowl.
18. Drizzle with the sauce mixture and serve.

Serving Suggestions: Serve with yogurt sauce.

Variation Tip: Thaw the vegetables completely before cooking.

Nutritional Information per Serving:

Calories: 443 | **Fat:** 16.4g|**Sat Fat:** 3.2g|**Carbohydrates:** 62.3g|**Fiber:** 3.6g|**Sugar:** 3.6g| **Protein:** 10.1g

Beans & Veggie Burgers

Preparation Time: 15 minutes
Cooking Time: 22 minutes
Servings: 4

Ingredients:

- 1 cup cooked black beans
- 2 cups boiled potatoes, peeled and mashed
- 1 cup fresh spinach, chopped
- 1 cup fresh mushrooms, chopped
- 2 teaspoons Chile lime seasoning
- Olive oil cooking spray

Preparation:

1. In a large bowl, add the beans, potatoes, spinach, mushrooms, and seasoning and with your hands, mix until well combined.
2. Make 4 equal-sized patties from the mixture.
3. Spray the patties with cooking spray evenly.
4. Press "Power Button" of Ninja Foodi Digital Air Fry Oven and turn the dial to select "Air Fry" mode.
5. Press "Time Button" and again turn the dial to set the cooking time to 22 minutes.
6. Now push "Temp Button" and rotate the dial to set the temperature at 370 degrees F.
7. Press "Start/Pause" button to start.
8. When the unit beeps to show that it is preheated, open the lid.
9. Arrange the patties in the greased air fry basket and insert in the oven.
10. When cooking time is completed, open the lid and
11. Flip the patties once after 12 minutes.

Serving Suggestions: Serve with avocado and tomato salad.

Variation Tip: Feel free to add seasoning of your choice.

Nutritional Information per Serving:

Calories: 113 | **Fat:** 0.4g|**Sat Fat:** 0g|**Carbohydrates:**23.1g|**Fiber:** 6.2g|**Sugar:** 1.7g| **Protein:** 6g

Spicy Potato

Preparation Time: 15 minutes
Cooking Time: 25 minutes
Servings: 4

Ingredients:

- 2 cups water
- 6 russet potatoes, peeled and cubed
- ½ tablespoon extra-virgin olive oil
- ½ of onion, chopped
- 1 tablespoon fresh rosemary, chopped
- 1 garlic clove, minced
- 1 jalapeño pepper, chopped
- ½ teaspoon garam masala powder
- ¼ teaspoon ground cumin
- ¼ teaspoon red chili powder
- Salt and ground black pepper, as required

Preparation:

1. In a large bowl, add the water and potatoes and set aside for about 30 minutes.
2. Drain well and pat dry with the paper towels.
3. In a bowl, add the potatoes and oil and toss to coat well.
4. Press "Power Button" of Ninja Foodi Digital Air Fry Oven and turn the dial to select "Air Fry" mode.
5. Press "Time Button" and again turn the dial to set the cooking time to 5 minutes.
6. Now push "Temp Button" and rotate the dial to set the temperature at 330 degrees F.
7. Press "Start/Pause" button to start.
8. When the unit beeps to show that it is preheated, open the lid.
9. Arrange the potato cubes in air fry basket and insert in the oven.
10. Remove from oven and transfer the potatoes into a bowl.
11. Add the remaining ingredients and toss to coat well.
12. Press "Power Button" of Ninja Foodi Digital Air Fry Oven and turn the dial to select "Air Fry" mode.
13. Press "Time Button" and again turn the dial to set the cooking time to 20 minutes.
14. Now push "Temp Button" and rotate the dial to set the temperature at 390 degrees F.
15. Press "Start/Pause" button to start.
16. When the unit beeps to show that it is preheated, open the lid.
17. Arrange the potato mixture in air fry basket and insert in the oven.
18. When cooking time is completed, open the lid and serve hot.

Serving Suggestions: Serve with plain bread.

Variation Tip: Adjust the ratio of spices.

Nutritional Information per Serving:

Calories: 274 | **Fat:** 2.3g|**Sat Fat:** 0.4g|**Carbohydrates:** 52.6g|**Fiber:** 8.5g|**Sugar:** 4.4g| **Protein:** 5.7g

Cheesy Kale

Preparation Time: 10 minutes
Cooking Time: 15 minutes
Servings: 3

Ingredients:

- 1 pound fresh kale, tough ribs removed and chopped
- 3 tablespoons olive oil
- Salt and ground black pepper, as required
- 1 cup goat cheese, crumbled
- 1 teaspoon fresh lemon juice

Preparation:

1. In a bowl, add the kale, oil, salt and black pepper and mix well.
2. Press "Power Button" of Ninja Foodi Digital Air Fry Oven and turn the dial to select "Air Fry" mode.
3. Press "Time Button" and again turn the dial to set the cooking time to 15 minutes.
4. Now push "Temp Button" and rotate the dial to set the temperature at 340 degrees F.
5. Press "Start/Pause" button to start.
6. When the unit beeps to show that it is preheated, open the lid and grease the air fry basket.
7. Arrange the kale into air fry basket and insert in the oven.
8. When cooking time is completed, open the lid and immediately transfer the kale mixture into a bowl.
9. Stir in the cheese and lemon juice and serve hot.

Serving Suggestions: Serve with a garnishing of lemon zest.

Variation Tip: Goat cheese can be replaced with feta.

Nutritional Information per Serving:

Calories: 327 | **Fat:** 24.7g|**Sat Fat:** 9.5g|**Carbohydrates:** 17.9g|**Fiber:** 2.3g|**Sugar:** 2.g| **Protein:** 11.6g

Parmesan Broccoli

Preparation Time: 10 minutes
Cooking Time: 15 minutes
Servings: 8

Ingredients:

- 2 pounds broccoli, cut into 1-inch florets
- 2 tablespoons butter
- Salt and ground black pepper, as required
- ¼ cup Parmesan cheese, grated

Preparation:

1. In a pan of boiling water, add the broccoli and cook for about 3-4 minutes.
2. Drain the broccoli well.
3. In a bowl, place the broccoli, cauliflower, oil, salt, and black pepper and toss to coat well.
4. Press "Power Button" of Ninja Foodi Digital Air Fry Oven and turn the dial to select "Air Fry" mode.
5. Press "Time Button" and again turn the dial to set the cooking time to 15 minutes.
6. Now push "Temp Button" and rotate the dial to set the temperature at 400 degrees F.
7. Press "Start/Pause" button to start.
8. When the unit beeps to show that it is preheated, open the lid.
9. Arrange the broccoli mixture in air fry basket and insert in the oven.
10. Toss the broccoli mixture once halfway through.
11. When cooking time is completed, open the lid and transfer the veggie mixture into a large bowl.
12. Immediately stir in the cheese and serve immediately.

Serving Suggestions: Serve with a drizzling of lemon juice.

Variation Tip: Choose broccoli heads with tight, green florets and firm stalks.

Nutritional Information per Serving:

Calories: 73 | **Fat:** 3.9g|**Sat Fat:** 2.1g|**Carbohydrates:** 7.5g|**Fiber:** 3g|**Sugar:** 1.9g| **Protein:** 4.2g

Caramelized Baby Carrots

Preparation Time: 10 minutes
Cooking Time: 15 minutes
Servings: 4

Ingredients:

- ½ cup butter, melted
- ½ cup brown sugar
- 1 pound bag baby carrots

Preparation:

1. In a bowl, mix together the butter, brown sugar and carrots.
2. Press "Power Button" of Ninja Foodi Digital Air Fry Oven and turn the dial to select "Air Fry" mode.
3. Press "Time Button" and again turn the dial to set the cooking time to 15 minutes.
4. Now push "Temp Button" and rotate the dial to set the temperature at 400 degrees F.
5. Press "Start/Pause" button to start.
6. When the unit beeps to show that it is preheated, open the lid.
7. Arrange the carrots in a greased air fry basket and insert in the oven.
8. When cooking time is completed, open the lid and serve warm.

Serving Suggestions: Serve with favorite greens.

Variation Tip: Make sure to pat dry the carrots before cooking.

Nutritional Information per Serving:

Calories: 312 | **Fat:** 23.2g|**Sat Fat:** 14.5g|**Carbohydrates:** 27.1g|**Fiber:** 3.3g|**Sugar:** 23g|**Protein:** 1g

Soy Sauce Green Beans

Preparation Time: 10 minutes
Cooking Time: 10 minutes
Servings: 2

Ingredients:

- 8 ounces fresh green beans, trimmed and cut in half
- 1 tablespoon soy sauce
- 1 teaspoon sesame oil

Preparation:

1. In a bowl, mix together the green beans, soy sauce and sesame oil.
2. Press "Power Button" of Ninja Foodi Digital Air Fry Oven and turn the dial to select "Air Fry" mode.
3. Press "Time Button" and again turn the dial to set the cooking time to 10 minutes.
4. Now push "Temp Button" and rotate the dial to set the temperature at 390 degrees F.
5. Press "Start/Pause" button to start.
6. When the unit beeps to show that it is preheated, open the lid.
7. Arrange the green beans in air fry basket and insert in the oven.
8. When cooking time is completed, open the lid and serve hot.

Serving Suggestions: Serve with the garnishing of sesame seeds.

Variation Tip: You can add seasoning of your choice.

Nutritional Information per Serving:

Calories: 62 | **Fat:** 2.6g|**Sat Fat:** 0.4g|**Carbohydrates:** 8.8g|**Fiber:** 4g|**Sugar:** 1.7g|**Protein:** 2.6g

Wine Braised Mushrooms

Preparation Time: 10 minutes
Cooking Time: 32minutes
Servings: 6

Ingredients:

- 1 tablespoon butter
- 2 teaspoons Herbs de Provence
- ½ teaspoon garlic powder
- 2 pounds fresh mushrooms, quartered
- 2 tablespoons white wine

Preparation:

1. In a frying pan, mix together the butter, Herbs de Provence, and garlic powder over medium-low heat and stir fry for about 2 minutes.
2. Stir in the mushrooms and remove from the heat.
3. Transfer the mushroom mixture into a baking pan.
4. Press "Power Button" of Ninja Foodi Digital Air Fry Oven and turn the dial to select "Air Fry" mode.
5. Press "Time Button" and again turn the dial to set the cooking time to 30 minutes.
6. Now push "Temp Button" and rotate the dial to set the temperature at 320 degrees F.
7. Press "Start/Pause" button to start.
8. When the unit beeps to show that it is preheated, open the lid.
9. Arrange the pan over the wire rack and insert in the oven.
10. After 25 minutes of cooking, stir the wine into mushroom mixture.
11. When cooking time is completed, open the lid and serve hot.

Serving Suggestions: Serve with a garnishing of fresh herbs.

Variation Tip: White wine can be replaced with broth.

Nutritional Information per Serving:

Calories: 54 | **Fat:** 2.4g|**Sat Fat:** 1.2g|**Carbohydrates:** 5.3g|**Fiber:** 1.5g|**Sugar:** 2.7g|
Protein: 4.8g

Fish & Seafood Recipes

Nuts Crusted Salmon

Preparation Time: 15 minutes
Cooking Time: 15 minutes
Servings: 2

Ingredients:

- 2 (6-ounce) skinless salmon fillets
- Salt and ground black pepper, as required
- 3 tablespoons walnuts, chopped finely
- 3 tablespoons quick-cooking oats, crushed
- 2 tablespoons olive oil

Preparation:

1. Rub the salmon fillets with salt and black pepper evenly.
2. In a bowl, mix together the walnuts, oats and oil.
3. Arrange the salmon fillets onto the greased sheet pan in a single layer.
4. Place the oat mixture over salmon fillets and gently, press down.
5. Press "Power Button" of Ninja Foodi Digital Air Fry Oven and turn the dial to select the "Air Bake" mode.
6. Press "Time Button" and again turn the dial to set the cooking time to 15 minutes.
7. Now push "Temp Button" and rotate the dial to set the temperature at 400 degrees F.
8. Press "Start/Pause" button to start.
9. When the unit beeps to show that it is preheated, open the lid.
10. Insert the sheet pan in oven.
11. When cooking time is completed, open the lid and serve hot.

Serving Suggestions: Serve with steamed asparagus.

Variation Tip: walnuts can be replaced with pecans.

Nutritional Information per Serving:

Calories: 446 | **Fat:** 319g|**Sat Fat:** 4g|**Carbohydrates:** 6.4g|**Fiber:** 1.6g|**Sugar:** 0.2g| **Protein:** 36.8g

Pesto Salmon

Preparation Time: 15 minutes
Cooking Time: 15 minutes
Servings: 4

Ingredients:

- 1¼ pound salmon fillet, cut into 4 fillets
- 2 tablespoons white wine
- 1 tablespoon fresh lemon juice
- 2 tablespoons pesto

Preparation:

1. Arrange the salmon fillets onto q foil-lined baking pan, skin-side down.
2. Drizzle the salmon fillets with wine and lemon juice.
3. Set aside for about 15 minutes.
4. Spread pesto over each salmon fillet evenly.
5. Press "Power Button" of Ninja Foodi Digital Air Fry Oven and turn the dial to select the "Air Broil" mode.
6. Press "Time Button" and again turn the dial to set the cooking time to 15 minutes.
7. Press "Start/Pause" button to start.
8. When the unit beeps to show that it is preheated, open the lid.
9. Insert the baking pan in oven.
10. When cooking time is completed, open the lid and serve hot.

Serving Suggestions: Serve with lemon slices.

Variation Tip: Fresh salmon should glisten, not look dull.

Nutritional Information per Serving:

Calories: 228 | **Fat:** 12g|**Sat Fat:** 1.9g|**Carbohydrates:** 0.8g|**Fiber:** 0.2g|**Sugar:** 0.6g| **Protein:** 28.3g

Cajun Salmon

Preparation Time: 10 minutes
Cooking Time: 7 minutes
Servings: 2

Ingredients:

- 2 (7-ounce) (¾-inch thick) salmon fillets
- 1 tablespoon Cajun seasoning
- ½ teaspoon sugar
- 1 tablespoon fresh lemon juice

Preparation:

1. Sprinkle the salmon fillets with Cajun seasoning and sugar evenly.
2. Press "Power Button" of Ninja Foodi Digital Air Fry Oven and turn the dial to select "Air Fry" mode.
3. Press "Time Button" and again turn the dial to set the cooking time to 7 minutes.
4. Now push "Temp Button" and rotate the dial to set the temperature at 356 degrees F.
5. Press "Start/Pause" button to start.
6. When the unit beeps to show that it is preheated, open the lid.
7. Arrange the salmon fillets, skin-side up in the greased air fry basket and insert in the oven.
8. When cooking time is completed, open the lid and transfer the salmon fillets onto a platter.
9. Drizzle with the lemon juice and serve hot.

Serving Suggestions: Serve with mashed cauliflower.

Variation Tip: Adjust the ratio of Cajun seasoning according to your taste.

Nutritional Information per Serving:

Calories: 268 | **Fat:** 12.3g|**Sat Fat:** 1.8g|**Carbohydrates:** 1.2g|**Fiber:** 0g|**Sugar:** 1.2g| **Protein:** 36.8g

Salmon Burgers

Preparation Time: 15 minutes
Cooking Time: 22 minutes
Servings: 6

Ingredients:

- 3 large russet potatoes, peeled and cubed
- 1 (6-ounce) cooked salmon fillet
- 1 egg
- ¾ cup frozen vegetables (of your choice), parboiled and drained
- 2 tablespoons fresh parsley, chopped
- 1 teaspoon fresh dill, chopped
- Salt and ground black pepper, as required
- 1 cup breadcrumbs
- ¼ cup olive oil

Preparation:

1. In a pan of boiling water, cook the potatoes for about 10 minutes.
2. Drain the potatoes well.
3. Transfer the potatoes into a bowl and mash with a potato masher.
4. Set aside to cool completely.
5. In another bowl, add the salmon and flake with a fork.
6. Add the cooked potatoes, egg, parboiled vegetables, parsley, dill, salt and black pepper and mix until well combined.
7. Make 6 equal-sized patties from the mixture.
8. Coat patties with breadcrumb evenly and then drizzle with the oil evenly.
9. Press "Power Button" of Ninja Foodi Digital Air Fry Oven and turn the dial to select "Air Fry" mode.
10. Press "Time Button" and again turn the dial to set the cooking time to 12 minutes.
11. Now push "Temp Button" and rotate the dial to set the temperature at 355 degrees F.
12. Press "Start/Pause" button to start.
13. When the unit beeps to show that it is preheated, open the lid.
14. Arrange the patties in greased air fry basket and insert in the oven.
15. Flip the patties once halfway through.
16. When cooking time is completed, open the lid and serve hot.

Serving Suggestions: Serve your favorite dipping sauce.

Variation Tip: You can use herbs of your choice in this recipe.

Nutritional Information per Serving:

Calories: 334 | **Fat:** 12.1g|**Sat Fat:** 2g|**Carbohydrates:** 45.2g|**Fiber:** 6.3g|**Sugar:** 4g|**Protein:** 12.5g

Buttered Trout

Preparation Time: 10 minutes
Cooking Time: 10 minutes
Servings: 2

Ingredients:

- 2 (6-ounces) trout fillets
- Salt and ground black pepper, as required
- 1 tablespoon butter, melted

Preparation:

1. Season each trout fillet with salt and black pepper and then coat with the butter.
2. Arrange the trout fillets onto the greased sheet pan in a single layer.
3. Press "Power Button" of Ninja Foodi Digital Air Fry Oven and turn the dial to select "Air Fry" mode.
4. Press "Time Button" and again turn the dial to set the cooking time to 10 minutes.
5. Now push "Temp Button" and rotate the dial to set the temperature at 360 degrees F.
6. Press "Start/Pause" button to start.
7. When the unit beeps to show that it is preheated, open the lid.
8. Insert the sheet pan in oven.
9. Flip the fillets once halfway through.
10. When cooking time is completed, open the lid and serve hot.

Serving Suggestions: Serve with your favorite salad.

Variation Tip: Rinse the trout thoroughly.

Nutritional Information per Serving:

Calories: 374 | **Fat:** 20.2g|**Sat Fat:** 6.2g|**Carbohydrates:** 0g|**Fiber:** 0g|**Sugar:** 0g| **Protein:** 45.4g

Crispy Cod

Preparation Time: 15 minutes
Cooking Time: 15 minutes
Servings: 4

Ingredients:

- 4 (4-ounce) (¾-inch thick) cod fillets
- Salt, as required
- 2 tablespoons all-purpose flour
- 2 eggs
- ½ cup panko breadcrumbs
- 1 teaspoon fresh dill, minced
- ½ teaspoon dry mustard
- ½ teaspoon lemon zest, grated
- ½ teaspoon onion powder
- ½ teaspoon paprika
- Olive oil cooking spray

Preparation

1. Season the cod fillets with salt generously.
2. In a shallow bowl, place the flour.
3. Crack the eggs in a second bowl and beat well.
4. In a third bowl, mix together the panko, dill, lemon zest, mustard and spices.
5. Coat each cod fillet with the flour, then dip into beaten eggs and finally, coat with panko mixture.
6. Press "Power Button" of Ninja Foodi Digital Air Fry Oven and turn the dial to select "Air Fry" mode.
7. Press "Time Button" and again turn the dial to set the cooking time to 15 minutes.
8. Now push "Temp Button" and rotate the dial to set the temperature at 400 degrees F.
9. Press "Start/Pause" button to start.
10. When the unit beeps to show that it is preheated, open the lid and grease the air fry basket.
11. Place the cod fillets into the prepared air fry basket and insert in the oven.
12. Flip the cod fillets once halfway through.
13. When cooking time is completed, open the lid and serve hot.

Serving Suggestions: Serve with steamed green beans.

Variation Tip: Make sure you remove all the fish scales before cooking.

Nutritional Information per Serving:

Calories: 190 | **Fat:** 4.3g|**Sat Fat:** 1.1g|**Carbohydrates:** 5.9g|**Fiber:** 0.4g|**Sugar:** 0.4g| **Protein:** 24g

Cod Parcel

Preparation Time: 10 minutes
Cooking Time: 23 minutes
Servings: 4

Ingredients:

- 2 (4-ounce) cod fillets
- 6 asparagus stalks
- ¼ cup white sauce
- 1 teaspoon oil
- ¼ cup champagne
- Salt and ground black pepper, as required

Preparation:

1. In a bowl, mix together all the ingredients.
2. Divide the cod mixture over 2 pieces of foil evenly.
3. Seal the foil around the cod mixture to form the packet.
4. Press "Power Button" of Ninja Foodi Digital Air Fry Oven and turn the dial to select "Air Fry" mode.
5. Press "Time Button" and again turn the dial to set the cooking time to 13 minutes.
6. Now push "Temp Button" and rotate the dial to set the temperature at 355 degrees F.
7. Press "Start/Pause" button to start.
8. When the unit beeps to show that it is preheated, open the lid.
9. Arrange the cod parcels in air fry basket and insert in the oven.
10. When cooking time is completed, open the lid and transfer the parcels onto serving plates.
11. Carefully unwrap the parcels and serve hot.

Serving Suggestions: Serve with mashed potatoes.

Variation Tip: The meat of cod should look fairly translucent.

Nutritional Information per Serving:

Calories: 188 | **Fat:** 6.6g|**Sat Fat:** 1.2g|**Carbohydrates:** 5g|**Fiber:** 0.8g|**Sugar:** 2.2g| **Protein:** 22.2g

Crispy Flounder

Preparation Time: 15 minutes
Cooking Time: 12 minutes
Servings: 3

Ingredients:

- 1 egg
- 1 cup dry Italian breadcrumbs
- ¼ cup olive oil
- 3 (6-ounce) flounder fillets

Preparation:

1. In a shallow bowl, beat the egg.
2. In another bowl, add the breadcrumbs and oil and mix until a crumbly mixture is formed.
3. Dip the flounder fillets into the beaten egg and then coat with the breadcrumb mixture.
4. Press "Power Button" of Ninja Foodi Digital Air Fry Oven and turn the dial to select "Air Fry" mode.
5. Press "Time Button" and again turn the dial to set the cooking time to 12 minutes.
6. Now push "Temp Button" and rotate the dial to set the temperature at 356 degrees F.
7. Press "Start/Pause" button to start.
8. When the unit beeps to show that it is preheated, open the lid and grease the air fry basket.
9. Place the flounder fillets into the prepared air fry basket and insert in the oven.
10. When cooking time is completed, open the lid and serve hot.

Serving Suggestions: Serve with potato chips.

Variation Tip: To avoid gluten, use crushed pork rinds instead of breadcrumbs.

Nutritional Information per Serving:

Calories: 508 | **Fat:** 22.8g|**Sat Fat:** 3.9g|**Carbohydrates:** 26.5g|**Fiber:** 1.8g|**Sugar:** 2.5g| **Protein:** 47.8g

Prawns in Butter Sauce

Preparation Time: 15 minutes
Cooking Time: 6 minutes
Servings: 2

Ingredients:

- ½ pound large prawns, peeled and deveined
- 1 large garlic clove, minced
- 1 tablespoon butter, melted
- 1 teaspoon fresh lemon zest, grated

Preparation:

1. In a bowl, add all the ingredients and toss to coat well.
2. Set aside at room temperature for about 30 minutes.
3. Arrange the prawn mixture into a baking pan.
4. Press "Power Button" of Ninja Foodi Digital Air Fry Oven and turn the dial to select "Air Bake" mode.
5. Press "Time Button" and again turn the dial to set the cooking time to 6 minutes.
6. Now push "Temp Button" and rotate the dial to set the temperature at 450 degrees F.
7. Press "Start/Pause" button to start.
8. When the unit beeps to show that it is preheated, open the lid.
9. Arrange the pan over the wire rack and insert in the oven.
10. When cooking time is completed, open the lid and serve immediately.

Serving Suggestions: Serve with fresh salad.

Variation Tip: Avoid shrimp that smells like ammonia.

Nutritional Information per Serving:

Calories: 189 | **Fat:** 7.7g|**Sat Fat:** 4.2g|**Carbohydrates:** 2.4g|**Fiber:** 0.1g|**Sugar:** 0.1g| **Protein:** 26g

Scallops with Capers Sauce

Preparation Time: 10 minutes
Cooking Time: 6 minutes
Servings: 2

Ingredients:

- 10 (1-ounce) sea scallops, cleaned and patted very dry
- Salt and ground black pepper, as required
- ¼ cup extra-virgin olive oil
- 2 tablespoons fresh parsley, finely chopped
- 2 teaspoons capers, finely chopped
- 1 teaspoon fresh lemon zest, finely grated
- ½ teaspoon garlic, finely chopped

Preparation:

1. Season each scallop evenly with salt and black pepper.
2. Press "Power Button" of Ninja Foodi Digital Air Fry Oven and turn the dial to select "Air Fry" mode.
3. Press "Time Button" and again turn the dial to set the cooking time to 6 minutes.
4. Now push "Temp Button" and rotate the dial to set the temperature at 400 degrees F.
5. Press "Start/Pause" button to start.
6. When the unit beeps to show that it is preheated, open the lid and grease the air fry basket.
7. Place the scallops into the prepared air fry basket and insert in the oven.
8. Meanwhile, for the sauce: in a bowl, mix the remaining ingredients.
9. When cooking time is completed, open the lid and transfer the scallops onto serving plates.
10. Top with the sauce and serve immediately.

Serving Suggestions: Serve with a garnishing of fresh herbs.

Variation Tip: Avoid shiny, wet or soft scallops.

Nutritional Information per Serving:

Calories: 344 | **Fat:** 26.3g|**Sat Fat:** 3.7g|**Carbohydrates:** 4.2g|**Fiber:** 0.3g|**Sugar:** 0.1g| **Protein:** 24g

Scallops with Spinach

Preparation Time: 15 minutes
Cooking Time: 10 minutes
Servings: 2

Ingredients:

- ¾ cup heavy whipping cream
- 1 tablespoon tomato paste
- 1 teaspoon garlic, minced
- 1 tablespoon fresh basil, chopped
- Salt and ground black pepper, as required
- 8 jumbo sea scallops
- Olive oil cooking spray
- 1 (12-ounces) package frozen spinach, thawed and drained

Preparation:

1. In a bowl, place the cream, tomato paste, garlic, basil, salt, and black pepper and mix well.
2. Spray each scallop evenly with cooking spray and then, sprinkle with a little salt and black pepper.
3. In the bottom of a baking pan, place the spinach.
4. Arrange scallops on top of the spinach in a single layer and top with the cream mixture evenly.
5. Press "Power Button" of Ninja Foodi Digital Air Fry Oven and turn the dial to select "Air Fry" mode.
6. Press "Time Button" and again turn the dial to set the cooking time to 10 minutes.
7. Now push "Temp Button" and rotate the dial to set the temperature at 350 degrees F.
8. Press "Start/Pause" button to start.
9. When the unit beeps to show that it is preheated, open the lid.
10. Place the pan into the prepared air fry basket and insert in the oven.
11. When cooking time is completed, open the lid and serve hot.

Serving Suggestions: Serve with crusty bread.

Variation Tip: Spinach can be replaced with kale.

Nutritional Information per Serving:

Calories: 309 | **Fat:** 18.8g|**Sat Fat:** 10.6g|**Carbohydrates:** 12.3g|**Fiber:** 4.1g|**Sugar:** 1.7g| **Protein:** 26.4g

Buttered Crab Shells

Preparation Time: 15 minutes
Cooking Time: 20 minutes
Servings: 4

Ingredients:

- 4 soft crab shells, cleaned
- 1 cup buttermilk
- 3 eggs
- 2 cups panko breadcrumb
- 2 teaspoons seafood seasoning
- 1½ teaspoons lemon zest, grated
- 2 tablespoons butter, melted

Preparations:

1. In a shallow bowl, place the buttermilk.
2. In a second bowl, whisk the eggs.
3. In a third bowl, mix together the breadcrumbs, seafood seasoning, and lemon zest.
4. Soak the crab shells into the buttermilk for about 10 minutes.
5. Now, dip the crab shells into beaten eggs and then, coat with the breadcrumbs mixture.
6. Press "Power Button" of Ninja Foodi Digital Air Fry Oven and turn the dial to select "Air Fry" mode.
7. Press "Time Button" and again turn the dial to set the cooking time to 10 minutes.
8. Now push "Temp Button" and rotate the dial to set the temperature at 375 degrees F.
9. Press "Start/Pause" button to start.
10. When the unit beeps to show that it is preheated, open the lid and grease the air fry basket.
11. Place the crab shells into the prepared air fry basket and insert in the oven.
12. When cooking time is completed, open the lid and transfer the crab shells onto serving plates.
13. Drizzle crab shells with the melted butter and serve immediately.

Serving Suggestions: Serve alongside the lemon slices.

Variation Tip: Use seasoning of your choice.

Nutritional Information per Serving:

Calories: 549 | **Fat:** 17.3g|**Sat Fat:** 7g|**Carbohydrates:** 11.5g|**Fiber:** 0.3g|**Sugar:** 3.3g| **Protein:** 53.5g

Poultry Mains Recipes

Herbed Cornish Game Hen

Preparation Time: 15 minutes
Cooking Time: 35 minutes
Servings: 4

Ingredients:

- 2 tablespoons avocado oil
- ½ teaspoon dried oregano
- ½ teaspoon dried rosemary
- ½ teaspoon dried thyme
- ½ teaspoon dried basil
- Salt and ground black pepper, as required
- 2 Cornish game hens

Preparations:

1. In a bowl, mix together the oil, dried herbs, salt and black pepper.
2. Rub each hen with herb mixture evenly.
3. Press "Power Button" of Ninja Foodi Digital Air Fry Oven and turn the dial to select "Air Fry" mode.
4. Press "Time Button" and again turn the dial to set the cooking time to 35 minutes.
5. Now push "Temp Button" and rotate the dial to set the temperature at 360 degrees F.
6. Press "Start/Pause" button to start.
7. When the unit beeps to show that it is preheated, open the lid and grease the air fry basket.
8. Arrange the hens into the prepared basket, breast side down and insert in the oven.
9. When cooking time is completed, open the lid and transfer the hens onto a platter.
10. Cut each hen in pieces and serve.

Serving Suggestions: Serve alongside roasted veggies.

Variation Tip: You can use fresh herbs instead of dried herbs.

Nutritional Information per Serving:

Calories: 895 | **Fat:** 62.9g|**Sat Fat:** 17.4g|**Carbohydrates:** 0.7g|**Fiber:** 0.5g|**Sugar:** 0g|**Protein:** 75.9g

Cajun Spiced Whole Chicken

Preparation Time: 15 minutes
Cooking Time: 1 hour 10 minutes
Servings: 6

Ingredients:

- ¼ cup butter, softened
- 2 teaspoons dried rosemary
- 2 teaspoons dried thyme
- 1 tablespoon Cajun seasoning
- 1 tablespoon onion powder
- 1 tablespoon garlic powder
- 1 tablespoon paprika
- 1 teaspoon cayenne pepper
- Salt, as required
- 1 (3-pound) whole chicken, neck and giblets removed

Preparation:

1. In a bowl, add the butter, herbs, spices and salt and mix well.
2. Rub the chicken with spicy mixture generously.
3. With kitchen twine, tie off wings and legs.
4. Press "Power Button" of Ninja Foodi Digital Air Fry Oven and turn the dial to select "Air Bake" mode.
5. Press "Time Button" and again turn the dial to set the cooking time to 70 minutes.
6. Now push "Temp Button" and rotate the dial to set the temperature at 380 degrees F.
7. Press "Start/Pause" button to start.
8. When the unit beeps to show that it is preheated, open the lid.
9. Arrange the chicken over the wire rack and insert in the oven.
10. When cooking time is completed, open the lid and place the chicken onto a platter for about 10 minutes before carving.
11. Cut into desired sized pieces and serve.

Serving Suggestions: Serve alongside a fresh green salad.

Variation Tip: You can adjust the ratio of spices according to your choice.

Nutritional Information per Serving:

Calories: 421 | **Fat:** 14.8g|**Sat Fat:** 6.9g|**Carbohydrates:** 2.3g|**Fiber:** 0.9g|**Sugar:** 0.5g|**Protein:** 66.3g

Lemony Whole Chicken

Preparation Time: 15 minutes
Cooking Time: 1 hour 20 minutes
Servings: 8

Ingredients:

- 1 (5-pound) whole chicken, neck and giblets removed
- Salt and ground black pepper, as required
- 2 fresh rosemary sprigs
- 1 small onion, peeled and quartered
- 1 garlic clove, peeled and cut in half
- 4 lemon zest slices
- 1 tablespoon extra-virgin olive oil
- 1 tablespoon fresh lemon juice

Preparation:

1. Rub the inside and outside of chicken with salt and black pepper evenly.
2. Place the rosemary sprigs, onion quarters, garlic halves and lemon zest in the cavity of the chicken.
3. With kitchen twine, tie off wings and legs.
4. Arrange the chicken onto a greased baking pan and drizzle with oil and lemon juice.
5. Press "Power Button" of Ninja Foodi Digital Air Fry Oven and turn the dial to select "Air Bake" mode.
6. Press "Time Button" and again turn the dial to set the cooking time to 20 minutes.
7. Now push "Temp Button" and rotate the dial to set the temperature at 400 degrees F.
8. Press "Start/Pause" button to start.
9. When the unit beeps to show that it is preheated, open the lid.
10. Arrange the pan over the wire rack and insert in the oven.
11. After 20 minutes of cooking, set the temperature to 375 degrees F for 60 minutes.
12. When cooking time is completed, open the lid and place the chicken onto a platter for about 10 minutes before carving.
13. Cut into desired sized pieces and serve.

Serving Suggestions: Serve alongside the steamed veggies.

Variation Tip: Lemon can be replaced with lime.

Nutritional Information per Serving:

Calories: 448 | **Fat:** 10.4g|**Sat Fat:** 2.7g|**Carbohydrates:** 1g|**Fiber:** 0.4g|**Sugar:** 0.2g| **Protein:** 82g

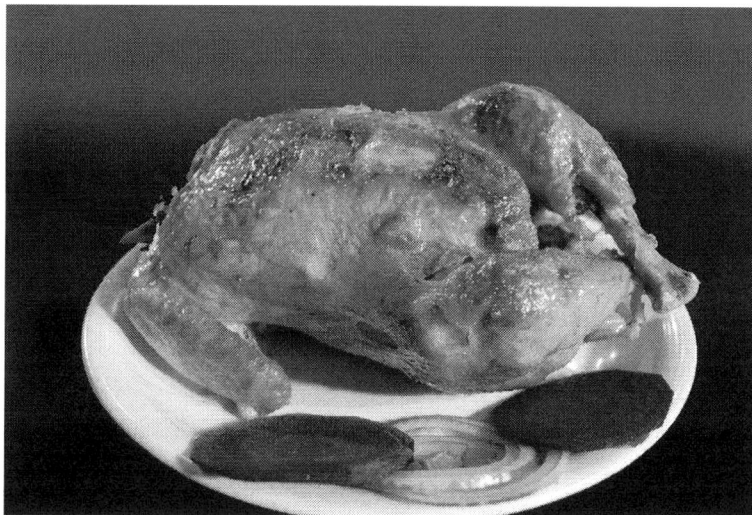

Crispy Chicken Legs

Preparation Time: 15 minutes
Cooking Time: 20 minutes
Servings: 3

Ingredients:

- 3 (8-ounce) chicken legs
- 1 cup buttermilk
- 2 cups white flour
- 1 teaspoon garlic powder
- 1 teaspoon onion powder
- 1 teaspoon ground cumin
- 1 teaspoon paprika
- Salt and ground black pepper, as required
- 1 tablespoon olive oil

Preparation:

1. In a bowl, place the chicken legs and buttermilk and refrigerate for about 2 hours.
2. In a shallow dish, mix together the flour and spices.
3. Remove the chicken from buttermilk.
4. Coat the chicken legs with flour mixture, then dip into buttermilk and finally, coat with the flour mixture again.
5. Press "Power Button" of Ninja Foodi Digital Air Fry Oven and turn the dial to select "Air Fry" mode.
6. Press "Time Button" and again turn the dial to set the cooking time to 20 minutes.
7. Now push "Temp Button" and rotate the dial to set the temperature at 355 degrees F.
8. Press "Start/Pause" button to start.
9. When the unit beeps to show that it is preheated, open the lid and grease the air fry basket.
10. Arrange chicken legs into the prepared air fry basket and drizzle with the oil.
11. Insert the basket in the oven.
12. When cooking time is completed, open the lid and serve hot.

Serving Suggestions: Serve with your favorite dip.

Variation Tip: White flour can be replaced with almond flour too.

Nutritional Information per Serving:

Calories: 817 | **Fat:** 23.3g|**Sat Fat:** 5.9g|**Carbohydrates:** 69.5g|**Fiber:** 2.7g|**Sugar:** 4.7g|**Protein:** 77.4g

Marinated Spicy Chicken Legs

Preparation Time: 10 minutes
Cooking Time: 20 minutes
Servings: 4

Ingredients:

- 4 chicken legs
- 3 tablespoons fresh lemon juice
- 3 teaspoons ginger paste
- 3 teaspoons garlic paste
- Salt, as required
- 4 tablespoons plain yogurt
- 2 teaspoons red chili powder
- 1 teaspoon ground cumin
- 1 teaspoon ground coriander
- 1 teaspoon ground turmeric
- Ground black pepper, as required

Preparation:

1. In a bowl, mix together the chicken legs, lemon juice, ginger, garlic and salt. Set aside for about 15 minutes.
2. Meanwhile, in another bowl, mix together the yogurt and spices.
3. Add the chicken legs and coat with the spice mixture generously.
4. Cover the bowl and refrigerate for at least 10-12 hours.
5. Press "Power Button" of Ninja Foodi Digital Air Fry Oven and turn the dial to select "Air Fry" mode.
6. Press "Time Button" and again turn the dial to set the cooking time to 20 minutes.
7. Now push "Temp Button" and rotate the dial to set the temperature at 440 degrees F.
8. Press "Start/Pause" button to start.
9. When the unit beeps to show that it is preheated, open the lid and grease the air fry basket.
10. Place the chicken legs into the prepared air fry basket and insert in the oven.
11. When cooking time is completed, open the lid and serve hot.

Serving Suggestions: Serve with fresh greens.

Variation Tip: Lemon juice can be replaced with vinegar.

Nutritional Information per Serving:

Calories: 461| **Fat:** 17.6g|**Sat Fat:** 5g|**Carbohydrates:** 4.3g|**Fiber:** 0.9g|**Sugar:** 1.5g| **Protein:** 67.1g

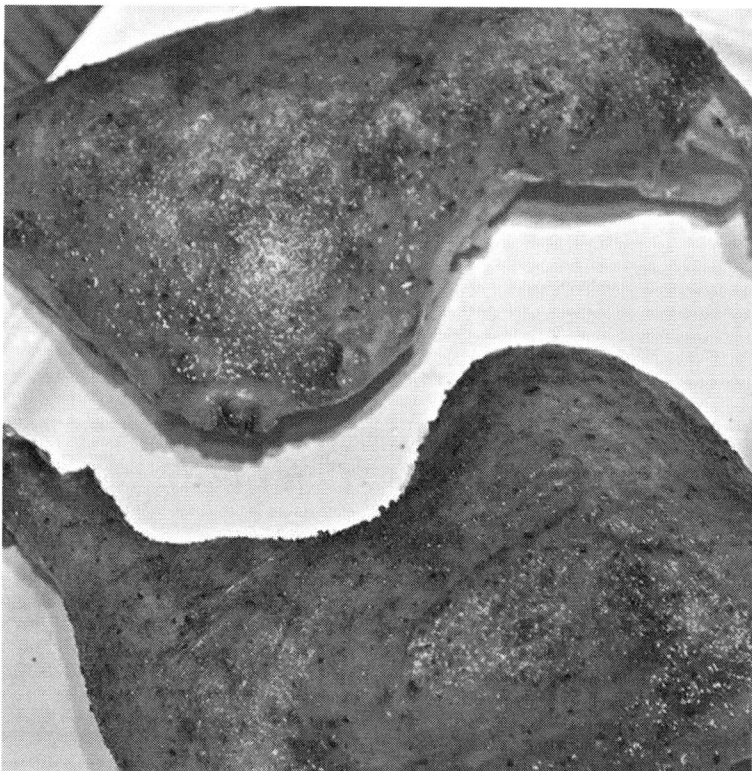

Gingered Chicken Drumsticks

Preparation Time: 10 minutes
Cooking Time: 25 minutes
Servings: 3

Ingredients:

- ¼ cup full-fat coconut milk
- 2 teaspoons fresh ginger, minced
- 2 teaspoons galangal, minced
- 2 teaspoons ground turmeric
- Salt, as required
- 3 (6-ounce) chicken drumsticks

Preparation:

1. Place the coconut milk, galangal, ginger, and spices in a large bowl and mix well.
2. Add the chicken drumsticks and coat with the marinade generously.
3. Refrigerate to marinate for at least 6-8 hours.
4. Press "Power Button" of Ninja Foodi Digital Air Fry Oven and turn the dial to select "Air Fry" mode.
5. Press "Time Button" and again turn the dial to set the cooking time to 25 minutes.
6. Now push "Temp Button" and rotate the dial to set the temperature at 375 degrees F.
7. Press "Start/Pause" button to start.
8. When the unit beeps to show that it is preheated, open the lid and grease the air fry basket.
9. Place the chicken drumsticks into the prepared air fry basket and insert in the oven.
10. When cooking time is completed, open the lid and serve hot.

Serving Suggestions: Serve alongside the lemony couscous.

Variation Tip: Coconut milk can be replaced with cream.

Nutritional Information per Serving:

Calories: 347 | **Fat:** 14.8g|**Sat Fat:** 6.9g|**Carbohydrates:** 3.8g|**Fiber:** 1.1g|**Sugar:** 0.8g|
Protein: 47.6g

Crispy Chicken Drumsticks

Preparation Time: 15 minutes
Cooking Time: 25 minutes
Servings: 4

Ingredients:

- 4 chicken drumsticks
- 1 tablespoon adobo seasoning
- Salt, as required
- 1 tablespoon onion powder
- 1 tablespoon garlic powder
- ½ tablespoon paprika
- Ground black pepper, as required
- 2 eggs
- 2 tablespoons milk
- 1 cup all-purpose flour
- ¼ cup cornstarch

Preparation:

1. Season chicken drumsticks with adobo seasoning and a pinch of salt.
2. Set aside for about 5minutes.
3. In a small bowl, add the spices, salt and black pepper and mix well.
4. In a shallow bowl, add the eggs, milk and 1 teaspoon of spice mixture and beat until well combined.
5. In another shallow bowl, add the flour, cornstarch and remaining spice mixture.
6. Coat the chicken drumsticks with flour mixture and tap off the excess.
7. Now, dip the chicken drumsticks in egg mixture.
8. Again coat the chicken drumsticks with flour mixture.
9. Arrange the chicken drumsticks onto a wire rack lined baking sheet and set aside for about 15 minutes.
10. Now, arrange the chicken drumsticks onto a sheet pan and spray the chicken with cooking spray lightly.
11. Press "Power Button" of Ninja Foodi Digital Air Fry Oven and turn the dial to select "Air Fry" mode.
12. Press "Time Button" and again turn the dial to set the cooking time to 25 minutes.
13. Now push "Temp Button" and rotate the dial to set the temperature at 350 degrees F.
14. Press "Start/Pause" button to start.
15. When the unit beeps to show that it is preheated, open the lid and grease the air fry basket.
16. Place the chicken drumsticks into the prepared air fry basket and insert in the oven.
17. When cooking time is completed, open the lid and serve hot.

Serving Suggestions: Serve with French fries.

Variation Tip: make sure to coat chicken pieces completely.

Nutritional Information per Serving:

Calories: 483 | **Fat:** 12.5g|**Sat Fat:** 3.4g|**Carbohydrates:** 35.1g|**Fiber:** 1.6g|**Sugar:** 1.8g| **Protein:** 53.7g

Lemony Chicken Thighs

Preparation Time: 15 minutes
Cooking Time: 20 minutes
Servings: 6

Ingredients:

- 6 (6-ounce) chicken thighs
- 2 tablespoons olive oil
- 2 tablespoons fresh lemon juice
- 1 tablespoon Italian seasoning
- Salt and ground black pepper, as required
- 1 lemon, sliced thinly

Preparation:

1. In a large bowl, add all the ingredients except for lemon slices and toss to coat well.
2. Refrigerate to marinate for 30 minutes to overnight.
3. Remove the chicken thighs and let any excess marinade drip off.
4. Press "Power Button" of Ninja Foodi Digital Air Fry Oven and turn the dial to select "Air Fry" mode.
5. Press "Time Button" and again turn the dial to set the cooking time to 20 minutes.
6. Now push "Temp Button" and rotate the dial to set the temperature at 350 degrees F.
7. Press "Start/Pause" button to start.
8. When the unit beeps to show that it is preheated, open the lid and grease the air fry basket.
9. Place the chicken thighs into the prepared air fry basket and insert in the oven.
10. After 10 minutes of cooking, flip the chicken thighs.
11. When cooking time is completed, open the lid and serve hot alongside the lemon slices.

Serving Suggestions: Serve alongside your favorite dipping sauce.

Variation Tip: Select chicken with a pinkish hue.

Nutritional Information per Serving:

Calories: 472 | **Fat:** 18g|**Sat Fat:** 4.3g|**Carbohydrates:** 0.6g|**Fiber:** 0.1g|**Sugar:** 0.4g| **Protein:** 49.3g

Chinese Chicken Drumsticks

Preparation Time: 10 minutes
Cooking Time: 20 minutes
Servings: 4

Ingredients:

- 1 tablespoon oyster sauce
- 1 teaspoon light soy sauce
- ½ teaspoon sesame oil
- 1 teaspoon Chinese five-spice powder
- Salt and ground white pepper, as required
- 4 (6-ounces) chicken drumsticks
- 1 cup cornflour

Preparation:

1. In a bowl, mix together the sauces, oil, five-spice powder, salt, and black pepper.
2. Add the chicken drumsticks and generously coat with the marinade.
3. Refrigerate for at least 30-40 minutes.
4. In a shallow dish, place the cornflour.
5. Remove the chicken from marinade and lightly coat with cornflour.
6. Press "Power Button" of Ninja Foodi Digital Air Fry Oven and turn the dial to select "Air Fry" mode.
7. Press "Time Button" and again turn the dial to set the cooking time to 20 minutes.
8. Now push "Temp Button" and rotate the dial to set the temperature at 390 degrees F.
9. Press "Start/Pause" button to start.
10. When the unit beeps to show that it is preheated, open the lid and grease the air fry basket.
11. Place the chicken drumsticks into the prepared air fry basket and insert in the oven.
12. When cooking time is completed, open the lid and serve hot.

Serving Suggestions: Serve with fresh greens.

Variation Tip: Use best quality sauces.

Nutritional Information per Serving:

Calories: 287 | **Fat:** 13.8g|**Sat Fat:** 7.1g|**Carbohydrates:** 1.6g|**Fiber:** 0.2g|**Sugar:** 0.1g| **Protein:** 38.3g

Crispy Chicken Thighs

Preparation Time: 15 minutes
Cooking Time: 25 minutes
Servings: 4

Ingredients:

- ½ cup all-purpose flour
- 1½ tablespoons Cajun seasoning
- 1 teaspoon seasoning salt
- 1 egg
- 4 (4-ounces) skin-on chicken thighs

Preparation:

1. In a shallow bowl, mix together the flour, Cajun seasoning, and salt.
2. In another bowl, crack the egg and beat well.
3. Coat each chicken thigh with the flour mixture, then dip into beaten egg and finally, coat with the flour mixture again.
4. Shake off the excess flour thoroughly.
5. Press "Power Button" of Ninja Foodi Digital Air Fry Oven and turn the dial to select "Air Fry" mode.
6. Press "Time Button" and again turn the dial to set the cooking time to 25 minutes.
7. Now push "Temp Button" and rotate the dial to set the temperature at 390 degrees F.
8. Press "Start/Pause" button to start.
9. When the unit beeps to show that it is preheated, open the lid and grease the air fry basket.
10. Place the chicken thighs into the prepared air fry basket and insert in the oven.
11. When cooking time is completed, open the lid and serve hot.

Serving Suggestions: Serve with ketchup.

Variation Tip: Feel free to use seasoning of your choice.

Nutritional Information per Serving:

Calories: 288 | **Fat:** 9.6g|**Sat Fat:** 2.7g|**Carbohydrates:** 12g|**Fiber:** 0.4g|**Sugar:** 0.1g| **Protein:** 35.9g

Oat Crusted Chicken Breasts

Preparation Time: 15 minutes
Cooking Time: 12 minutes
Servings: 2

Ingredients:

- 2 (6-ounce) chicken breasts
- Salt and ground black pepper, as required
- ¾ cup oats
- 2 tablespoons mustard powder
- 1 tablespoon fresh parsley
- 2 medium eggs

Preparation:

1. Place the chicken breasts onto a cutting board and with a meat mallet, flatten each into even thickness.
2. Then, cut each breast in half.
3. Sprinkle the chicken pieces with salt and black pepper and set aside.
4. In a blender, add the oats, mustard powder, parsley, salt and black pepper and pulse until a coarse breadcrumb-like mixture is formed.
5. Transfer the oat mixture into a shallow bowl.
6. In another bowl, crack the eggs and beat well.
7. Coat the chicken with oats mixture and then, dip into beaten eggs and again, coat with the oats mixture.
8. Press "Power Button" of Ninja Foodi Digital Air Fry Oven and turn the dial to select "Air Fry" mode.
9. Press "Time Button" and again turn the dial to set the cooking time to 12 minutes.
10. Now push "Temp Button" and rotate the dial to set the temperature at 350 degrees F.
11. Press "Start/Pause" button to start.
12. When the unit beeps to show that it is preheated, open the lid and grease the air fry basket.
13. Place the chicken breasts into the prepared air fry basket and insert in the oven.
14. Flip the chicken breasts once halfway through.
15. When cooking time is completed, open the lid and serve hot.

Serving Suggestions: Serve with mashed potatoes.

Variation Tip: Check the meat "best by" date.

Nutritional Information per Serving:

Calories: 556 | **Fat:** 22.2g|**Sat Fat:** 5.3g|**Carbohydrates:** 25.1g|**Fiber:** 4.8g|**Sugar:** 1.4g| **Protein:** 61.6g

Crispy Chicken Cutlets

Preparation Time: 15 minutes
Cooking Time: 30 minutes
Servings: 4

Ingredients:

- ¾ cup flour
- 2 large eggs
- 1½ cups breadcrumbs
- ¼ cup Parmesan cheese, grated
- 1 tablespoon mustard powder
- Salt and ground black pepper, as required
- 4 (6-ounces) (¼-inch thick) skinless, boneless chicken cutlets

Preparation:

1. In a shallow bowl, add the flour.
2. In a second bowl, crack the eggs and beat well.
3. In a third bowl, mix together the breadcrumbs, cheese, mustard powder, salt, and black pepper.
4. Season the chicken with salt, and black pepper.
5. Coat the chicken with flour, then dip into beaten eggs and finally coat with the breadcrumbs mixture.
6. Press "Power Button" of Ninja Foodi Digital Air Fry Oven and turn the dial to select "Air Fry" mode.
7. Press "Time Button" and again turn the dial to set the cooking time to 30 minutes.
8. Now push "Temp Button" and rotate the dial to set the temperature at 355 degrees F.
9. Press "Start/Pause" button to start.
10. When the unit beeps to show that it is preheated, open the lid and grease the air fry basket.
11. Place the chicken cutlets into the prepared air fry basket and insert in the oven.
12. When cooking time is completed, open the lid and serve hot.

Serving Suggestions: Serve with favorite greens.

Variation Tip: Parmesan cheese can be replaced with your favorite cheese.

Nutritional Information per Serving:

Calories: 526 | **Fat:** 13g|**Sat Fat:** 4.2g|**Carbohydrates:** 48.6g|**Fiber:** 3g|**Sugar:** 3g| **Protein:** 51.7g

Brie Stuffed Chicken Breasts

Preparation Time: 15 minutes
Cooking Time: 15 minutes
Servings: 4

Ingredients:

- 2 (8-ounce) skinless, boneless chicken fillets
- Salt and ground black pepper, as required
- 4 brie cheese slices
- 1 tablespoon fresh chive, minced
- 4 bacon slices

Preparation:

1. Cut each chicken fillet in 2 equal-sized pieces.
2. Carefully, make a slit in each chicken piece horizontally about ¼-inch from the edge.
3. Open each chicken piece and season with salt and black pepper.
4. Place 1 cheese slice in the open area of each chicken piece and sprinkle with chives.
5. Close the chicken pieces and wrap each one with a bacon slice.
6. Secure with toothpicks.
7. Press "Power Button" of Ninja Foodi Digital Air Fry Oven and turn the dial to select "Air Fry" mode.
8. Press "Time Button" and again turn the dial to set the cooking time to 15 minutes.
9. Now push "Temp Button" and rotate the dial to set the temperature at 355 degrees F.
10. Press "Start/Pause" button to start.
11. When the unit beeps to show that it is preheated, open the lid and grease the air fry basket.
12. Place the chicken pieces into the prepared air fry basket and insert in the oven.
13. When cooking time is completed, open the lid and place the rolled chicken breasts onto a cutting board.
14. Cut into desired-sized slices and serve.

Serving Suggestions: Serve with creamy mashed potatoes.

Variation Tip: Season the chicken breasts slightly.

Nutritional Information per Serving:

Calories: 394 | **Fat:** 24g|**Sat Fat:** 10.4g|**Carbohydrates:** 0.6g|**Fiber:** 0g|**Sugar:** 0.1g| **Protein:** 42g

Chicken Kabobs

Preparation Time: 15 minutes
Cooking Time: 9 minutes
Servings: 2

Ingredients:

- 1 (8-ounce) chicken breast, cut into medium-sized pieces
- 1 tablespoon fresh lemon juice
- 3 garlic cloves, grated
- 1 tablespoon fresh oregano, minced
- ½ teaspoon lemon zest, grated
- Salt and ground black pepper, as required
- 1 teaspoon plain Greek yogurt
- 1 teaspoon olive oil

Preparation:

1. In a large bowl, add the chicken, lemon juice, garlic, oregano, lemon zest, salt and black pepper and toss to coat well.
2. Cover the bowl and refrigerate overnight.
3. Remove the bowl from the refrigerator and stir in the yogurt and oil.
4. Thread the chicken pieces onto the metal skewers.
5. Press "Power Button" of Ninja Foodi Digital Air Fry Oven and turn the dial to select "Air Fry" mode.
6. Press "Time Button" and again turn the dial to set the cooking time to 9 minutes.
7. Now push "Temp Button" and rotate the dial to set the temperature at 350 degrees F.
8. Press "Start/Pause" button to start.
9. When the unit beeps to show that it is preheated, open the lid and grease the air fry basket.
10. Place the skewers into the prepared air fry basket and insert in the oven.
11. Flip the skewers once halfway through.
12. When cooking time is completed, open the lid and serve hot.

Serving Suggestions: Serve alongside fresh salad.

Variation Tip: Make sure to tri the chicken pieces.

Nutritional Information per Serving:

Calories: 167 | **Fat:** 5.5g|**Sat Fat:** 0.5g|**Carbohydrates:** 3.4g|**Fiber:** 0.5g|**Sugar:** 1.1g| **Protein:** 24.8g

Simple Turkey Breast

Preparation Time: 10 minutes
Cooking Time: 1 hour 20 minutes
Servings: 6

Ingredients:

- 1 (2¾-pound) bone-in, skin-on turkey breast half
- Salt and ground black pepper, as required

Preparation:

1. Rub the turkey breast with the salt and black pepper evenly.
2. Arrange the turkey breast into a greased baking pan.
3. Press "Power Button" of Ninja Foodi Digital Air Fry Oven and turn the dial to select "Air Bake" mode.
4. Press "Time Button" and again turn the dial to set the cooking time to 1 hour 20 minutes.
5. Now push "Temp Button" and rotate the dial to set the temperature at 450 degrees F.
6. Press "Start/Pause" button to start.
7. When the unit beeps to show that it is preheated, open the lid.
8. Arrange the pan over the wire rack and insert in the oven.
9. When cooking time is completed, open the lid and place the turkey breast onto a cutting board.
10. With a piece of foil, cover the turkey breast for about 20 minutes before slicing.
11. With a sharp knife, cut the turkey breast into desired size slices and serve.

Serving Suggestions: Serve alongside the steamed veggies.

Variation Tip: Beware of flat spots on meat, which can indicate thawing and refreezing.

Nutritional Information per Serving:

Calories: 221 | **Fat:** 0.8g|**Sat Fat:** 0g|**Carbohydrates:** 0g|**Fiber:** 0g|**Sugar:** 0g| **Protein:** 51.6g

Herbed Duck Breast

Preparation Time: 15 minutes
Cooking Time: 20 minutes
Servings: 2

Ingredients:

- 1 (10-ounce) duck breast
- Olive oil cooking spray
- ½ tablespoon fresh thyme, chopped
- ½ tablespoon fresh rosemary, chopped
- 1 cup chicken broth
- 1 tablespoon fresh lemon juice
- Salt and ground black pepper, as required

Preparation:

1. Spray the duck breast with cooking spray evenly.
2. In a bowl, mix well the remaining ingredients.
3. Add the duck breast and coat with the marinade generously.
4. Refrigerate, covered for about 4 hours.
5. With a piece of foil, cover the duck breast
6. Press "Power Button" of Ninja Foodi Digital Air Fry Oven and turn the dial to select "Air Fry" mode.
7. Press "Time Button" and again turn the dial to set the cooking time to 15 minutes.
8. Now push "Temp Button" and rotate the dial to set the temperature at 390 degrees F.
9. Press "Start/Pause" button to start.
10. When the unit beeps to show that it is preheated, open the lid and grease the air fry basket.
11. Place the duck breast into the prepared air fry basket and insert in the oven.
12. After 15 minutes of cooking, set the temperature to 355 degrees F for 5 minutes.
13. When cooking time is completed, open the lid and serve hot.

Serving Suggestions: Serve with spiced potatoes.

Variation Tip: Don't undercook the duck meat.

Nutritional Information per Serving:

Calories: 209 | **Fat:** 6.6g|**Sat Fat:** 0.3g|**Carbohydrates:** 1.6g|**Fiber:** 0.6g|**Sugar:** 0.5g| **Protein:** 33.8g

Beef, Pork & Lamb Recipes

Simple Beef Tenderloin

Preparation Time: 10 minutes
Cooking Time: 50 minutes
Servings: 10

Ingredients:

- 1 (3½-pound) beef tenderloin, trimmed
- 2 tablespoons olive oil
- Salt and ground black pepper, as required

Preparation:

1. With kitchen twine, tie the tenderloin.
2. Rub the tenderloin with oil and season with salt and black pepper.
3. Place the tenderloin into the greased baking pan.
4. Press "Power Button" of Ninja Foodi Digital Air Fry Oven and turn the dial to select the "Air Roast" mode.
5. Press "Time Button" and again turn the dial to set the cooking time to 50 minutes.
6. Now push "Temp Button" and rotate the dial to set the temperature at 400 degrees F.
7. Press "Start/Pause" button to start.
8. When the unit beeps to show that it is preheated, open the lid and insert the baking pan in the oven.
9. When cooking time is completed, open the lid and place the tenderloin onto a platter for about 10 minutes before slicing.
10. With a sharp knife, cut the tenderloin into desired sized slices and serve.

Serving Suggestions: Serve with lemony herbed couscous.

Variation Tip: Make sure to trim the meat before cooking.

Nutritional Information per Serving:

Calories: 351 | **Fat:** 17.3g|**Sat Fat:** 5.9g|**Carbohydrates:** 0g|**Fiber:** 0g|**Sugar:** 0g|
Protein: .46g

Herbed Chuck Roast

Preparation Time: 10 minutes
Cooking Time: 45 minutes
Servings: 6

Ingredients:

- 1 (2-pound) beef chuck roast
- 1 tablespoon olive oil
- 1 teaspoon dried rosemary, crushed
- 1 teaspoon dried thyme, crushed
- Salt, as required

Preparation:

1. In a bowl, add the oil, herbs and salt and mix well.
2. Coat the beef roast with herb mixture generously.
3. Arrange the beef roast onto the greased cooking pan.
4. Press "Power Button" of Ninja Foodi Digital Air Fry Oven and turn the dial to select "Air Fry" mode.
5. Press "Time Button" and again turn the dial to set the cooking time to 45 minutes.
6. Now push "Temp Button" and rotate the dial to set the temperature at 360 degrees F.
7. Press "Start/Pause" button to start.
8. When the unit beeps to show that it is preheated, open the lid and insert the baking pan in the oven.
9. When cooking time is completed, open the lid and place the roast onto a cutting board.
10. With a piece of foil, cover the beef roast for about 20 minutes before slicing.
11. With a sharp knife, cut the beef roast into desired size slices and serve.

Serving Suggestions: Serve with roasted Brussels sprouts.

Variation Tip: Dried hers can be replaced with fresh herbs.

Nutritional Information per Serving:

Calories: 304 | **Fat:** 14g|**Sat Fat:** 4.5g|**Carbohydrates:** 0.2g|**Fiber:** 0.2g|**Sugar:** 0g| **Protein:** 41.5g

Seasoned Sirloin Steak

Preparation Time: 10 minutes
Cooking Time: 12 minutes
Servings: 2

Ingredients:

- 2 (7-ounce) top sirloin steaks
- 1 tablespoon steak seasoning
- Salt and ground black pepper, as required

Preparation:

1. Season each steak with steak seasoning, salt and black pepper.
2. Arrange the steaks onto the greased cooking pan.
3. Press "Power Button" of Ninja Foodi Digital Air Fry Oven and turn the dial to select "Air Fry" mode.
4. Press "Time Button" and again turn the dial to set the cooking time to 12 minutes.
5. Now push "Temp Button" and rotate the dial to set the temperature at 400 degrees F.
6. Press "Start/Pause" button to start.
7. When the unit beeps to show that it is preheated, open the lid and insert the baking pan in the oven.
8. Flip the steaks once halfway through.
9. When cooking time is completed, open the lid and serve hot.

Serving Suggestions: Serve with cheesy scalloped potatoes.

Variation Tip: The surface of the steak should be moist but not wet or sticky.

Nutritional Information per Serving:

Calories: 369 | **Fat:** 12.4g|**Sat Fat:** 4.7g|**Carbohydrates:** 0g|**Fiber:** 0g|**Sugar:** 0g| **Protein:** 60.2g

Steak with Bell Peppers

Preparation Time: 15 minutes
Cooking Time: 11 minutes
Servings: 4

Ingredients:

- 1 teaspoon dried oregano, crushed
- 1 teaspoon onion powder
- 1 teaspoon garlic powder
- 1 teaspoon red chili powder
- 1 teaspoon paprika
- Salt, as required
- 1¼ pounds flank steak, cut into thin strips
- 3 green bell peppers, seeded and cubed
- 1 red onion, sliced
- 2 tablespoons olive oil
- 3-4 tablespoons feta cheese, crumbled

Preparation:

1. In a large bowl, mix together the oregano and spices.
2. Add the steak strips, bell peppers, onion, and oil and mix until well combined.
3. Press "Power Button" of Ninja Foodi Digital Air Fry Oven and turn the dial to select "Air Fry" mode.
4. Press "Time Button" and again turn the dial to set the cooking time to 11 minutes.
5. Now push "Temp Button" and rotate the dial to set the temperature at 390 degrees F.
6. Press "Start/Pause" button to start.
7. When the unit beeps to show that it is preheated, open the lid and grease the air fry basket.
8. Place the steak mixture into the prepared air fry basket and insert in the oven.
9. When cooking time is completed, open the lid and transfer the steak mixture onto serving plates.
10. Serve immediately with the topping of feta.

Serving Suggestions: Serve with plain rice.

Variation Tip: Adjust the ratio of spices according to your taste.

Nutritional Information per Serving:

Calories: 732 | **Fat:** 35g|**Sat Fat:** 12.9g|**Carbohydrates:** 11.5g|**Fiber:** 2.5g|**Sugar:** 6.5g|**Protein:** 89.3g

Spiced Pork Shoulder

Preparation Time: 15 minutes
Cooking Time: 55 minutes
Servings: 4

Ingredients:

- 1 teaspoon ground cumin
- 1 teaspoon cayenne pepper
- ½ teaspoon garlic powder
- ½ teaspoon onion powder
- Salt and ground black pepper, as required
- 2 pounds skin-on pork shoulder

Preparation:

1. In a small bowl, place the spices, salt and black pepper and mix well.
2. Arrange the pork shoulder onto a cutting board, skin-side down.
3. Season the inner side of pork shoulder with salt and black pepper.
4. With kitchen twines, tie the pork shoulder into a long round cylinder shape.
5. Season the outer side of pork shoulder with spice mixture.
6. Press "Power Button" of Ninja Foodi Digital Air Fry Oven and turn the dial to select the "Air Roast" mode.
7. Press "Time Button" and again turn the dial to set the cooking time to 55 minutes.
8. Now push "Temp Button" and rotate the dial to set the temperature at 350 degrees F.
9. Press "Start/Pause" button to start.
10. When the unit beeps to show that it is preheated, open the lid and grease the air fry basket.
11. Arrange the pork shoulder into air fry basket and insert in the oven.
12. When cooking time is completed, open the lid and place the pork shoulder onto a platter for about 10 minutes before slicing.
13. With a sharp knife, cut the pork shoulder into desired sized slices and serve.

Serving Suggestions: Serve with southern-style grits.

Variation Tip: Choose a pork shoulder with pinkish-red color.

Nutritional Information per Serving:

Calories: 445 | **Fat:** 32.5g|**Sat Fat:** 11.9g|**Carbohydrates:** 0.7g|**Fiber:** 0.2g|**Sugar:** 0.2g| **Protein:** 35.4g

Bacon-Wrapped Pork Tenderloin

Preparation Time: 15 minutes
Cooking Time: 30minutes
Servings: 4

Ingredients:

- 1 (1½ pound) pork tenderloin
- 2 tablespoons Dijon mustard
- 1 tablespoon honey
- 4 bacon strips

Preparation:

1. Coat the tenderloin with mustard and honey.
2. Wrap the pork tenderloin with bacon strips.
3. Press "Power Button" of Ninja Foodi Digital Air Fry Oven and turn the dial to select "Air Fry" mode.
4. Press "Time Button" and again turn the dial to set the cooking time to 30 minutes.
5. Now push "Temp Button" and rotate the dial to set the temperature at 360 degrees F.
6. Press "Start/Pause" button to start.
7. When the unit beeps to show that it is preheated, open the lid and grease the air fry basket.
8. Place the pork tenderloin into the prepared air fry basket and insert in the oven.
9. Flip the pork tenderloin once halfway through.
10. When cooking time is completed, open the lid and place the pork loin onto a cutting board for about 10 minutes before slicing.
11. With a sharp knife, cut the tenderloin into desired sized slices and serve.

Serving Suggestions: Enjoy with mashed potatoes.

Variation Tip: Make sure to remove the silver skin from the tenderloin.

Nutritional Information per Serving:

Calories: 386 | **Fat:** 16.1g|**Sat Fat:** 5.7g|**Carbohydrates:** 4.8g|**Fiber:** 0.3g|**Sugar:** 4.4g|
Protein: 52g

Breaded Pork Chops

Preparation Time: 15 minutes
Cooking Time: 15 minutes
Servings: 3

Ingredients:

- 3 (6-ounce) pork chops
- Salt and ground black pepper, as required
- ¼ cup plain flour
- 1 egg
- 4 ounces seasoned breadcrumbs
- 1 tablespoon canola oil

Preparation:

1. Season each pork chop with salt and black pepper.
2. In a shallow bowl, place the flour
3. In a second bowl, crack the egg and beat well.
4. In a third bowl, add the breadcrumbs and oil and mix until a crumbly mixture forms.
5. Coat the pork chop with flour, then dip into beaten egg and finally, coat with the breadcrumbs mixture.
6. Press "Power Button" of Ninja Foodi Digital Air Fry Oven and turn the dial to select "Air Fry" mode.
7. Press "Time Button" and again turn the dial to set the cooking time to 15 minutes.
8. Now push "Temp Button" and rotate the dial to set the temperature at 400 degrees F.
9. Press "Start/Pause" button to start.
10. When the unit beeps to show that it is preheated, open the lid and grease the air fry basket.
11. Place the lamb chops into the prepared air fry basket and insert in the oven.
12. Flip the chops once halfway through.
13. When cooking time is completed, open the lid and serve hot

Serving Suggestions: Serve with your favorite dipping sauce.

Variation Tip: Don't cook chops straight from the refrigerator

Nutritional Information per Serving:

Calories: 413 | **Fat:** 20.2g|**Sat Fat:** 4.4g|**Carbohydrates:** 31g|**Fiber:** 1.6g|**Sugar:** 0.1g| **Protein:** 28.3g

Pork Stuffed Bell Peppers

Preparation Time: 20 minutes
Cooking Time: 1 hour 10 minutes
Servings: 4

Ingredients:

- 4 medium green bell peppers
- 2/3 pound ground pork
- 2 cups cooked white rice
- 1½ cups marinara sauce, divided
- 1 teaspoon Worcestershire sauce
- 1 teaspoon Italian seasoning
- Salt and ground black pepper, as required
- ½ cup mozzarella cheese, shredded

Preparation:

1. Cut the tops from bell peppers and then carefully remove the seeds.
2. Heat a large skillet over medium heat and cook the pork for bout 6-8 minutes, breaking into crumbles.
3. Add the rice, ¾ cup of marinara sauce, Worcestershire sauce, Italian seasoning, salt and black pepper and stir to combine.
4. Remove from the heat.
5. Arrange the bell peppers into the greased baking pan.
6. Carefully, stuff each bell pepper with the pork mixture and top each with the remaining sauce.
7. Press "Power Button" of Ninja Foodi Digital Air Fry Oven and turn the dial to select the "Air Bake" mode.
8. Press "Time Button" and again turn the dial to set the cooking time to 60 minutes.
9. Now push "Temp Button" and rotate the dial to set the temperature at 350 degrees F.
10. Press "Start/Pause" button to start.
11. When the unit beeps to show that it is preheated, open the lid.
12. Insert the baking pan in oven.
13. After 50 minute of cooking, top each bell pepper with cheese.
14. When cooking time is completed, open the lid and transfer the bell peppers onto a platter.
15. Serve warm.

Serving Suggestions: Serve with baby greens.

Variation Tip: Use best quality ground pork.

Nutritional Information per Serving:

Calories: 580 | **Fat:** 7.1g|**Sat Fat:** 2.2g|**Carbohydrates:** 96.4g|**Fiber:** 5.2g|**Sugar:** 14.8g|**Protein:** 30.3g

Rosemary Lamb Chops

Preparation Time: 10 minutes
Cooking Time: 6 minutes
Servings: 2

Ingredients:

- 1 tablespoon olive oil, divided
- 2 garlic cloves, minced
- 1 tablespoon fresh rosemary, chopped
- Salt and ground black pepper, as required
- 4 (4-ounce) lamb chops

Preparation:

1. In a large bowl, mix together the oil, garlic, rosemary, salt and black pepper.
2. Coat the chops with half of the garlic mixture.
3. Press "Power Button" of Ninja Foodi Digital Air Fry Oven and turn the dial to select "Air Fry" mode.
4. Press "Time Button" and again turn the dial to set the cooking time to 6 minutes.
5. Now push "Temp Button" and rotate the dial to set the temperature at 390 degrees F.
6. Press "Start/Pause" button to start.
7. When the unit beeps to show that it is preheated, open the lid and grease the air fry basket.
8. Place the lamb chops into the prepared air fry basket and insert in the oven.
9. Flip the chops once halfway through.
10. When cooking time is completed, open the lid and serve hot with the topping of the remaining garlic mixture.

Serving Suggestions: Serve with yogurt sauce.

Variation Tip: Lamb chops that has dried out edges and does not smell fresh should not be purchased.

Nutritional Information per Serving:

Calories: 492 | **Fat:** 23.9g|**Sat Fat:** 7.1g|**Carbohydrates:** 2.1g|**Fiber:** 0.8g|**Sugar:** 0g| **Protein:** 64g

Garlicky Lamb Steaks

Preparation Time: 15 minutes
Cooking Time: 15 minutes
Servings: 4

Ingredients:

- ½ onion, roughly chopped
- 5 garlic cloves, peeled
- 1 tablespoon fresh ginger, peeled
- 1 teaspoon ground fennel
- ½ teaspoon ground cumin
- ½ teaspoon ground cinnamon
- ½ teaspoon cayenne pepper
- Salt and ground black pepper, as required
- 1½ pounds boneless lamb sirloin steaks

Preparation:

1. In a blender, add the onion, garlic, ginger, and spices and pulse until smooth.
2. Transfer the mixture into a large bowl.
3. Add the lamb steaks and coat with the mixture generously.
4. Refrigerate to marinate for about 24 hours.
5. Press "Power Button" of Ninja Foodi Digital Air Fry Oven and turn the dial to select "Air Fry" mode.
6. Press "Time Button" and again turn the dial to set the cooking time to 15 minutes.
7. Now push "Temp Button" and rotate the dial to set the temperature at 330 degrees F.
8. Press "Start/Pause" button to start.
9. When the unit beeps to show that it is preheated, open the lid and grease the air fry basket.
10. Place the lamb steaks into the prepared air fry basket and insert in the oven.
11. Flip the steaks once halfway through.
12. When cooking time is completed, open the lid and serve hot.

Serving Suggestions: Serve with your favorite greens.

Variation Tip: Allow the lamb steaks to reach room temperature before cooking.

Nutritional Information per Serving:

Calories: 336 | **Fat:** 12.8g|**Sat Fat:** 4.5g|**Carbohydrates:** 4.2g|**Fiber:** 1g|**Sugar:** 0.7g|**Protein:** 8.4g

Herbs Crumbed Rack of Lamb

Preparation Time: 15 minutes
Cooking Time: 30 minutes
Servings: 5

Ingredients:

- 1 tablespoon butter, melted
- 1 garlic clove, finely chopped
- 1¾ pounds rack of lamb
- Salt and ground black pepper, as required
- 1 egg
- ½ cup panko breadcrumbs
- 1 tablespoon fresh thyme, minced
- 1 tablespoon fresh rosemary, minced

Preparation:

1. In a bowl, mix together the butter, garlic, salt, and black pepper.
2. Coat the rack of lamb evenly with garlic mixture.
3. In a shallow dish, beat the egg.
4. In another dish, mix together the breadcrumbs and herbs.
5. Dip the rack of lamb in beaten egg and then coat with breadcrumbs mixture.
6. Press "Power Button" of Ninja Foodi Digital Air Fry Oven and turn the dial to select "Air Fry" mode.
7. Press "Time Button" and again turn the dial to set the cooking time to 25 minutes.
8. Now push "Temp Button" and rotate the dial to set the temperature at 212 degrees F.
9. Press "Start/Pause" button to start.
10. When the unit beeps to show that it is preheated, open the lid and grease the air fry basket.
11. Place the rack of lamb into the prepared air fry basket and insert in the oven.
12. After 25 minutes of cooking,
13. When cooking time is completed, open the lid and set the temperature at 390 degrees F for 5 minutes.
14. When cooking time is completed, open the lid and place the rack of lamb onto a cutting board for about 5-10 minutes.
15. With a sharp knife, cut the rack of lamb into individual chops and serve.

Serving Suggestions: Serve with a drizzling of lemon juice.

Variation Tip: Make sure to rest the rack of lamb before cutting into chops.

Nutritional Information per Serving:

Calories: 331 | **Fat:** 17.2g|**Sat Fat:** 6.7g|**Carbohydrates:** 2.6g|**Fiber:** 0.5g|**Sugar:** 0g| **Protein:** 32.7g

Lamb Burgers

Preparation Time: 10 minutes
Cooking Time: 8 minutes
Servings: 6

Ingredients:

- 2 pounds ground lamb
- ½ tablespoon onion powder
- ½ tablespoon garlic powder
- ¼ teaspoon ground cumin
- Salt and ground black pepper, as required

Preparation:

1. In a bowl, add all the ingredients and mix well.
2. Make 6 equal-sized patties from the mixture.
3. Arrange the patties onto the greased sheet pan in a single layer.
4. Press "Power Button" of Ninja Foodi Digital Air Fry Oven and turn the dial to select "Air Fry" mode.
5. Press "Time Button" and again turn the dial to set the cooking time to 8 minutes.
6. Now push "Temp Button" and rotate the dial to set the temperature at 360 degrees F.
7. Press "Start/Pause" button to start.
8. When the unit beeps to show that it is preheated, open the lid.
9. Insert the sheet pan in oven.
10. Flip the burgers once halfway through.
11. When cooking time is completed, open the lid and serve hot.

Serving Suggestions: Serve with fresh salad.

Variation Tip: For the best result, grind your meat at home.

Nutritional Information per Serving:

Calories: 286 | **Fat:** 11.1g|**Sat Fat:** 4g|**Carbohydrates:** 1g|**Fiber:** 0.1g|**Sugar:** 0.4g| **Protein:** 42.7g

Dessert Recipes

Honeyed Banana

Preparation Time: 10 minutes
Cooking Time: 10 minutes
Servings: 2

Ingredients:

- 1 ripe banana, peeled and sliced lengthwise
- ½ teaspoon fresh lemon juice
- 2 teaspoons honey
- 1/8 teaspoon ground cinnamon

Preparation:

1. Coat each banana half with lemon juice.
2. Arrange the banana halves onto the greased sheet pan cut sides up.
3. Drizzle the banana halves with honey and sprinkle with cinnamon.
4. Press "Power Button" of Ninja Foodi Digital Air Fry Oven and turn the dial to select "Air Fry" mode.
5. Press "Time Button" and again turn the dial to set the cooking time to 10 minutes.
6. Now push "Temp Button" and rotate the dial to set the temperature at 350 degrees F.
7. Press "Start/Pause" button to start.
8. When the unit beeps to show that it is preheated, open the lid.
9. Insert the sheet pan in oven.
10. When cooking time is completed, open the lid and transfer the banana slices onto a platter.
11. Serve immediately.

Serving Suggestions: Serve with garnishing of almonds.

Variation Tip: Honey can be replaced with maple syrup.

Nutritional Information per Serving:

Calories: 74 | **Fat:** 0.2g|**Sat Fat:** 0.1g|**Carbohydrates:** 19.4g|**Fiber:** 1.6g|**Sugar:** 13g| **Protein:** 0.7g

Chocolate Bites

Preparation Time: 15 minutes
Cooking Time: 13 minutes
Servings: 8

Ingredients:

- 2 cups plain flour
- 2 tablespoons cocoa powder
- ½ cup icing sugar
- Pinch of ground cinnamon
- 1 teaspoon vanilla extract
- ¾ cup chilled butter
- ¼ cup chocolate, chopped into 8 chunks

Preparation:

1. In a bowl, mix together the flour, icing sugar, cocoa powder, cinnamon and vanilla extract.
2. With a pastry cutter, cut the butter and mix till a smooth dough forms.
3. Divide the dough into 8 equal-sized balls.
4. Press 1 chocolate chunk in the center of each ball and cover with the dough completely.
5. Place the balls into the baking pan.
6. Press "Power Button" of Ninja Foodi Air Fry Digital Oven and turn the dial to select the "Air Fry" mode.
7. Press "Time Button" and again turn the dial to set the cooking time to 8 minutes.
8. Now push "Temp Button" and rotate the dial to set the temperature at 355 degrees F.
9. Press "Start/Pause" button to start.
10. When the unit beeps to show that it is preheated, open the lid.
11. Arrange the pan in air fry basket and insert in the oven.
12. After 8 minutes of cooking, set the temperature at 320 degrees F for 5 minutes.
13. When cooking time is completed, open the lid and place the baking pan onto the wire rack to cool completely before serving.

Serving Suggestions: Serve with a sprinkling of coconut shreds.

Variation Tip: Use best quality cocoa powder.

Nutritional Information per Serving:

Calories: 328 | **Fat:** 19.3g|**Sat Fat:** 12.2g|**Carbohydrates:** 35.3g|**Fiber:** 1.4g|
Sugar: 10.2g|**Protein:** 4.1g

Shortbread Fingers

Preparation Time: 15 minutes
Cooking Time: 12 minutes
Servings: 10

Ingredients:

- 1/3 cup caster sugar
- 1 2/3 cups plain flour
- ¾ cup butter

Preparation:

1. In a large bowl, mix together the sugar and flour.
2. Add the butter and mix until a smooth dough forms.
3. Cut the dough into 10 equal-sized fingers.
4. With a fork, lightly prick the fingers.
5. Place the fingers into the lightly greased baking pan.
6. Press "Power Button" of Ninja Foodi Digital Air Fry Oven and turn the dial to select "Air Fry" mode.
7. Press "Time Button" and again turn the dial to set the cooking time to 12 minutes.
8. Now push "Temp Button" and rotate the dial to set the temperature at 355 degrees F.
9. Press "Start/Pause" button to start.
10. When the unit beeps to show that it is preheated, open the lid.
11. Arrange the pan in air fry basket and insert in the oven.
12. When cooking time is completed, open the lid and place the baking pan onto a wire rack to cool for about 5-10 minutes.
13. Now, invert the shortbread fingers onto the wire rack to completely cool before serving.

Serving Suggestions: Serve with a dusting of powdered sugar.

Variation Tip: For best result, chill the dough in the refrigerator for 30 minutes before cooking.

Nutritional Information per Serving:

Calories: 223 | **Fat:** 14g|**Sat Fat:** 8.8g|**Carbohydrates:** 22.6g|**Fiber:** 0.6g|**Sugar:** 0.7g| **Protein:** 2.3g

Apple Pastries

Preparation Time: 15 minutes
Cooking Time: 10minutes
Servings: 6

Ingredients:

- ½ of large apple, peeled, cored and chopped
- 1 teaspoon fresh orange zest, grated finely
- ½ tablespoon white sugar
- ½ teaspoon ground cinnamon
- 7.05 ounce prepared frozen puff pastry

Preparation:

1. In a bowl, mix together all ingredients except puff pastry.
2. Cut the pastry in 16 squares.
3. Place about a teaspoon of the apple mixture in the center of each square.
4. Fold each square into a triangle and press the edges slightly with wet fingers.
5. Then with a fork, press the edges firmly.
6. Press "Power Button" of Ninja Foodi Digital Air Fry Oven and turn the dial to select "Air Fry" mode.
7. Press "Time Button" and again turn the dial to set the cooking time to 10 minutes.
8. Now push "Temp Button" and rotate the dial to set the temperature at 390 degrees F.
9. Press "Start/Pause" button to start.
10. When the unit beeps to show that it is preheated, open the lid.
11. Arrange the pastries in the greased air fry basket and insert in the oven.
12. When cooking time is completed, open the lid and transfer the pastries onto a platter.
13. Serve warm.

Serving Suggestions: Serve with a dusting of powdered sugar.

Variation Tip: Use sweet apple.

Nutritional Information per Serving:

Calories: 198 | **Fat:** 12.7g|**Sat Fat:** 3.2g|**Carbohydrates:** 18.8g|**Fiber:** 1.1g|**Sugar:** 3.2g| **Protein:** 2.5g

Vanilla Soufflé

Preparation Time: 15 minutes
Cooking Time: 23 minutes
Servings: 6

Ingredients:

- ¼ cup butter, softened
- ¼ cup all-purpose flour
- ½ cup plus 2 tablespoons sugar, divided
- 1 cup milk
- 3 teaspoons vanilla extract, divided
- 4 egg yolks
- 5 egg whites
- 1 teaspoon cream of tartar
- 2 tablespoons powdered sugar plus extra for dusting

Preparation:

1. In a bowl, add the butter, and flour and mix until a smooth paste forms.
2. In a medium pan, mix together ½ cup of sugar and milk over medium-low heat and cook for about 3 minutes or until the sugar is dissolved, stirring continuously.
3. Add the flour mixture, whisking continuously and simmer for about 3-4 minutes or until mixture becomes thick.
4. Remove from the heat and stir in 1 teaspoon of vanilla extract.
5. Set aside for about 10 minutes to cool.
6. In a bowl, add the egg yolks and 1 teaspoon of vanilla extract and mix well.
7. Add the egg yolk mixture into milk mixture and mix until well combined.
8. In another bowl, add the egg whites, cream of tartar, remaining sugar, and vanilla extract and with a wire whisk, beat until stiff peaks form.
9. Fold the egg whites mixture into milk mixture.
10. Grease 6 ramekins and sprinkle each with a pinch of sugar.
11. Place mixture into the prepared ramekins and with the back of a spoon, smooth the top surface.
12. Press "Power Button" of Ninja Foodi Digital Air Fry Oven and turn the dial to select "Air Fry" mode.
13. Press "Time Button" and again turn the dial to set the cooking time to 16 minutes.
14. Now push "Temp Button" and rotate the dial to set the temperature at 330 degrees F.
15. Press "Start/Pause" button to start.
16. When the unit beeps to show that it is preheated, open the lid.
17. Arrange the ramekins in air fry basket and insert in the oven.
18. When cooking time is completed, open the lid and place the ramekins onto a wire rack to cool slightly.

19. Sprinkle with the powdered sugar and serve warm.

Serving Suggestions: Serve with caramel sauce.

Variation Tip: Room temperature eggs will get the best results.

Nutritional Information per Serving:

Calories: 250 | **Fat:** 11.6g|**Sat Fat:** 6.5g|**Carbohydrates:** 29.8g|**Fiber:** o.1g|**Sugar:** 25g|
Protein: 6.8g

Blueberry Muffins

Preparation Time: 15 minutes
Cooking Time: 20 minutes
Servings: 6

Ingredients:

- 1 egg, beaten
- 1 ripe banana, peeled and mashed
- 1¼ cups almond flour
- 2 tablespoons granulated sugar
- ½ teaspoon baking powder
- 1 tablespoon coconut oil, melted
- 1/8 cup maple syrup
- 1 teaspoon apple cider vinegar
- 1 teaspoon vanilla extract
- 1 teaspoon lemon zest, grated
- Pinch of ground cinnamon
- ½ cup fresh blueberries

Preparation:

1. In a large bowl, add all the ingredients except for blueberries and mix until well combined.
2. Gently fold in the blueberries.
3. Grease a 6 cups muffin pan.
4. Place the mixture into prepared muffin cups about ¾ full.
5. Press "Power Button" of Ninja Foodi Digital Air Fry Oven and turn the dial to select "Air Bake" mode.
6. Press "Time Button" and again turn the dial to set the cooking time to 12 minutes.
7. Now push "Temp Button" and rotate the dial to set the temperature at 375 degrees F.
8. Press "Start/Pause" button to start.
9. When the unit beeps to show that it is preheated, open the lid.
10. Arrange the muffin pan over the wire rack and insert in the oven.
11. When cooking time is completed, open the lid and place the muffin molds onto a wire rack to cool for about 10 minutes.
12. Carefully invert the muffins onto the wire rack to completely cool before serving.

Serving Suggestions: Serve with a hot cup of coffee.

Variation Tip: Make sure to use ripened blueberries.

Nutritional Information per Serving:

Calories: 223 | **Fat:** 14.8g|**Sat Fat:** 3g|**Carbohydrates:** 20.1g|**Fiber:** 3.4g|**Sugar:** 12.5g|**Protein:** 6.2g

Nutella Banana Muffins

Preparation Time: 15 minutes
Cooking Time: 25 minutes
Servings: 12

Ingredients:

- 1 2/3 cups plain flour
- 1 teaspoon baking soda
- 1 teaspoon baking powder
- 1 teaspoon ground cinnamon
- ¼ teaspoon salt
- 4 ripe bananas, peeled and mashed
- 2 eggs
- ½ cup brown sugar
- 1 teaspoon vanilla essence
- 3 tablespoons milk
- 1 tablespoon Nutella
- ¼ cup walnuts

Preparation:

1. Grease 12 muffin molds. Set aside.
2. In a large bowl, sift together the flour, baking soda, baking powder, cinnamon, and salt.
3. In another bowl, mix together the remaining ingredients except walnuts.
4. Add the banana mixture into flour mixture and mix until just combined.
5. Fold in the walnuts.
6. Place the mixture into the prepared muffin molds.
7. Press "Power Button" of Ninja Foodi Digital Air Fry Oven and turn the dial to select "Air Fry" mode.
8. Press "Time Button" and again turn the dial to set the cooking time to 25 minutes.
9. Now push "Temp Button" and rotate the dial to set the temperature at 250 degrees F.
10. Press "Start/Pause" button to start.
11. When the unit beeps to show that it is preheated, open the lid.
12. Arrange the muffin molds in air fry basket and insert in the oven.
13. When cooking time is completed, open the lid and place the muffin molds onto a wire rack to cool for about 10 minutes.
14. Carefully, invert the muffins onto the wire rack to completely cool before serving.

Serving Suggestions: Enjoy with a glass of milk.

Variation Tip: Have all ingredients at room temperature before you start making the batter.

Nutritional Information per Serving:

Calories: 227 | **Fat:** 6.6g|**Sat Fat:** 1.5g|**Carbohydrates:** 38.1g|**Fiber:** 2.4g|**Sugar:** 15.8g| **Protein:** 5.2g

Fudge Brownies

Preparation Time: 15 minutes
Cooking Time: 20 minutes
Servings: 8

Ingredients:

- 1 cup sugar
- ½ cup butter, melted
- ½ cup flour
- 1/3 cup cocoa powder
- 1 teaspoon baking powder
- 2 eggs
- 1 teaspoon vanilla extract

Preparation:

1. Grease a baking pan.
2. In a large bowl, add the sugar and butter and whisk until light and fluffy.
3. Add the remaining ingredients and mix until well combined.
4. Place mixture into the prepared pan and with the back of a spatula, smooth the top surface.
5. Press "Power Button" of Ninja Foodi Digital Air Fry Oven and turn the dial to select "Air Fry" mode.
6. Press "Time Button" and again turn the dial to set the cooking time to 20 minutes.
7. Now push "Temp Button" and rotate the dial to set the temperature at 350 degrees F.
8. Press "Start/Pause" button to start.
9. When the unit beeps to show that it is preheated, open the lid.
10. Arrange the pan in air fry basket and insert in the oven.
11. When cooking time is completed, open the lid and place the baking pan onto a wire rack to cool completely.
12. Cut into 8 equal-sized squares and serve.

Serving Suggestions: Serve with a drizzling of melted chocolate.

Variation Tip: Choose good quality ingredients.

Nutritional Information per Serving:

Calories: 250 | **Fat:** 13.2g|**Sat Fat:** 7.9g|**Carbohydrates:** 33.4g|**Fiber:** 1.3g|**Sugar:** 25.2g| **Protein:** 3g

Cherry Clafoutis

Preparation Time: 15 minutes
Cooking Time: 25 minutes
Servings: 4

Ingredients:

- 1½ cups fresh cherries, pitted
- 3 tablespoons vodka
- ¼ cup flour
- 2 tablespoons sugar
- Pinch of salt
- ½ cup sour cream
- 1 egg
- 1 tablespoon butter
- ¼ cup powdered sugar

Preparation:

1. In a bowl, mix together the cherries and vodka.
2. In another bowl, mix together the flour, sugar, and salt.
3. Add the sour cream, and egg and mix until a smooth dough forms.
4. Grease a cake pan.
5. Place flour mixture evenly into the prepared cake pan.
6. Spread cherry mixture over the dough.
7. Place butter on top in the form of dots.
8. Press "Power Button" of Ninja Foodi Digital Air Fry Oven and turn the dial to select "Air Fry" mode.
9. Press "Time Button" and again turn the dial to set the cooking time to 25 minutes.
10. Now push "Temp Button" and rotate the dial to set the temperature at 355 degrees F.
11. Press "Start/Pause" button to start.
12. When the unit beeps to show that it is preheated, open the lid.
13. Arrange the pan in air fry basket and insert in the oven.
14. When cooking time is completed, open the lid and place the pan onto a wire rack to cool for about 10-15 minutes before serving.
15. Now, invert the Clafoutis onto a platter and sprinkle with powdered sugar.
16. Cut the Clafoutis into desired sized slices and serve warm.

Serving Suggestions: Serve with a topping of whipped cream.

Variation Tip: Replace vodka with kirsch.

Nutritional Information per Serving:

Calories: 241 | **Fat:** 10.1g|**Sat Fat:** 5.9g|**Carbohydrates:** 29g|**Fiber:** 1.3g|**Sugar:** 20.6g| **Protein:** 3.9g

21 Days Meal Plan

Day 1:

Breakfast: Sweet & Spiced Toasts

Lunch: Stuffed Zucchini

Dinner: Herbed Cornish Game Hen

Day 2:

Breakfast: Parmesan Eggs in Avocado Cups

Lunch: Salmon Burgers

Dinner: Simple Beef Tenderloin

Day 3:

Breakfast: Potato & Corned Beef Casserole

Lunch: Veggie Rice

Dinner: Lemony Chicken Thighs

Day 4:

Breakfast: Cloud Eggs

Lunch: Tofu in Sweet & Sour Sauce

Dinner: Nuts Crusted Salmon

Day 5:

Breakfast: Savory Parsley Soufflé

Lunch: Lamb Burgers

Dinner: Pork Stuffed Bell Peppers

Day 6:

Breakfast: Date Bread

Lunch: Scallops with Capers Sauce

Dinner: Herbs Crumbed Rack of Lamb

Day 7:

Breakfast: Sweet & Spiced Toasts

Lunch: Tofu with Broccoli

Dinner: Gingered Chicken Drumsticks

Day 8:

Breakfast: Savory Sausage & Beans Muffins

Lunch: Scallops with Capers Sauce

Dinner: Simple Turkey Breast

Day 9:

Breakfast: Mushroom Frittata

Lunch: Prawns in Butter Sauce

Dinner: Bacon-Wrapped Pork Tenderloin

Day 10:

Breakfast: Savory Parsley Soufflé

Lunch: Chicken Kabobs

Dinner: Buttered Trout

Day 11:

Breakfast: Date Bread

Lunch: Stuffed Zucchini

Dinner: Cod Parcel

Day 12:

Breakfast: Bacon, Spinach & Egg Cups

Lunch: Beans & Veggie Burgers

Dinner: Chinese Chicken Drumsticks

Day 13:

Breakfast: Cloud Eggs

Lunch: Tofu in Sweet & Sour Sauce

Dinner: Breaded Pork Chops

Day 14:

Breakfast: Simple Bread

Lunch: Scallops with Spinach

Dinner: Oat Crusted Chicken Breasts

Day 15:

Breakfast: Potato & Corned Beef Casserole

Lunch: Lamb Burgers

Dinner: Brie Stuffed Chicken Breasts

Day 16:

Breakfast: Savory Sausage & Beans Muffins

Lunch: Chicken Kabobs

Dinner: Herbed Chuck Roast

Day 17:

Breakfast: Mushroom Frittata

Lunch: Salmon Burgers

Dinner: Steak with Bell Peppers

Day 18:

Breakfast: Savory Parsley Soufflé

Lunch: Beans & Veggie Burgers

Dinner: Cajun Salmon

Day 19:

Breakfast: Bacon, Spinach & Egg Cups

Lunch: Veggie Rice

Dinner: Rosemary Lamb Chops

Day 20:

Breakfast: Parmesan Eggs in Avocado Cups

Lunch: Prawns in Butter Sauce

Dinner: Seasoned Sirloin Steak

Day 21:

Breakfast: Simple Bread

Lunch: Tofu with Broccoli

Dinner: Lemony Whole Chicken

Conclusion

The Ninja Foodi Digital Air Fry Oven is, without a doubt, perfect for your kitchen. It offers many cooking functions like air broiling, toasting, baking, dehydrating, keeping your food warm, air roasting, and of course, air frying. The control panel of the device is digital and can be easily used without any ambiguities. It performs all these functions very profoundly and is very reasonable for its price value. It only has a prominent shortcoming that it cannot fit in a complete chicken. However, this factor is easily dominated by the performance it offers in all the cooking functions.

Made in the USA
Monee, IL
20 August 2021